Advance Praise for *Business Engineering with Object Techno*

"We confidently predict that Taylor's *Business Engineering with Object Technology* will be the hottest OO book in 1995 and will lead lots of people to rethink what they assume about how one might link business analysis and object technology."

—PAUL HARMON
Editor
November Issue,
Object-Oriented Strategies

"A new, powerful methodology which will enable business people to apply innovative concepts to optimize their enterprises. Should become a best seller."

—TED KULIGOWSKI
U.S. Information Agency

"My consulting practice has been searching for a methodology to enable a consultant to sit down with a client and begin to model the business with objects. This book represents a conceptual breakthrough, pointing the way to the future. It is an answer to a prayer. I predict that it will become a seminal reference in our field."

—MICHAEL J. RAMSEY
Consultant
IBM Consulting Group

"David Taylor effectively distills the critical success factors required for reengineering the organization through object technology in a refreshingly clear and understandable manner. This book is a manifesto for both managers and developers seeking to use object technology to lead their organizations to competitive advantage."

—DAVID NEWMAN
President
Techneum, Inc.

"This book presents a very powerful and easily understandable approach to integrating business process reengineering with object technology. The *convergent engineering* approach goes a long way towards solving the problem of building reusable business objects. A must read if you are trying to understand the new world of objects."

—DILLON RIDGUARD
Principal, OO Competency Center
IBM Consulting Group

Business Engineering with Object Technology

DAVID A. TAYLOR, PhD

John Wiley & Sons, Inc.
New York • Chichester • Brisbane • Toronto • Singapore

Publisher: Katherine Schowalter
Senior Editor: Diane D. Cerra
Managing Editor: Robert S. Aronds
Editorial Production & Design: North Market Street Graphics

Designations used by companies to distinguish their products are often claimed as trademarks. In all instances where John Wiley & Sons, Inc. is aware of a claim, the product names appear in initial capital or all capital letters. Readers, however, should contact the appropriate companies for more complete information regarding trademarks and registration.

This text is printed on acid-free paper.

This publication is designed to provide accurate and authoritative information in regard to the subject matter covered. It is sold with the understanding that the publisher is not engaged in rendering legal, accounting, or other professional service. If legal advice or other expert assistance is required, the services of a competent professional person should be sought.

Library of Congress Cataloging-in-Publication Data:

Taylor, David A., 1943-
    Business engineering with object technology / David A. Taylor.
        p.   cm.
    Includes bibliographical references.
    ISBN 0-471-04521-7 (pbk. : acid-free paper)
    1. Object-oriented programming. 2. Business—Data processing.
    I. Title.
    QA76.64.T39   1995
    658.4'038'011—dc20
                                                    94-36369
                                                         CIP

Printed in the United States of America
10 9 8 7 6 5 4 3 2 1

CONTENTS

We stand on the threshold of a new era in business engineering. For the first time in the history of computers, it is now possible to build information systems that directly reflect and expand the way we think about business processes. The critical enabler for this transformation is object technology.

This book presents a systematic methodology for gaining competitive advantage through object-oriented business systems. I call this methodology convergent engineering *because it merges business engineering and software engineering into a unified discipline. The output of convergent engineering is an object-oriented business model that represents both an organization and its supporting software. Unlike conventional business systems, this model integrates, simulates, and executes organizational processes across an enterprise. Moreover, it can evolve over time to support continuous process improvement.*

Convergent engineering has been under development for nearly 10 years. I first formulated the vision when I was building object-oriented manufacturing systems in the mid-1980s. I refined and extended its concepts over the course of five years as a consultant helping Fortune 500 companies manage the adoption of object technology. I formed Enterprise Engines Inc. in the spring of 1991 in order to introduce the methodology to a broader audience. With the help of my colleagues and clients, the methodology has matured to the point where it is ready for wide-scale adoption.

This book is the distillation of a decade of theoretical analysis and real-world experience. It offers a proven approach to achieving new levels of corporate adaptability and sustained competitive advantage. I wish you every success in your adoption of convergent engineering.

A C K N O W L E D G M E N T S

First and always, I would like to express my deepest appreciation to my wife, Nina. Steadfast friend, patient ally, wise counselor, and sustaining inspiration, she is a most beloved life partner.

Next, I would like to offer my profound thanks to the following people at Enterprise Engines. Steven Forgey and John Churin provided critical insights that helped transform a vision into a viable methodology, and it is hard to imagine a better pair of partners with whom to share this exciting undertaking. Michael and Jacob Taylor not only used their considerable programming talents to validate the concepts in this book, they also proved that it is still possible to mix family and business to the betterment of both. Susanna Yu spent countless hours transforming my sketches into professional illustrations, and Lori Hurwitz provided the unfailing support we all needed to get this book into production.

I would also like to thank the people who were kind enough to review earlier versions of this book: Vic Ahmed at CresSoft, Charles Bacon at the Novum Group, Barney Barnett at Barnett & Associates, Cheryl Dietz at Resource Integration Associates, David Gale at IBM, Michael Kleeman at the Boston Consulting Group, Ted Kuligowski at the U.S. Information Agency, Ken Mayers at Mayers Associates, Doug McCausland at MCI, Kurt McMillen at Boeing Computer Services, Toni Nessi at EDS, David Newman at Techneum, Marick Payton at Stanford University, Michael Ramsey at IBM, Dillon Ridguard at IBM, Tom Robben at J.P. Morgan, Teri Roberts at MadenTech Consulting, Jeff Thompson at U.S. West, and Tom Vayda at Vayda Consulting.

Finally, I would like to thank our clients, past and present, who provided the formidable array of real-world business problems that allowed us to validate and refine the techniques of convergent engineering.

PART ONE

Foundation

1

Engineering
an Organization

In order to survive in an increasingly competitive business environment, companies must be willing to reinvent themselves on a continuous basis. They can do this only if their software support systems are capable of rapid change. This is rarely the case, and many organizations are locked in place by catatonic information systems. Convergent engineering, as defined in this book, offers a new opportunity to create more flexible, adaptive business systems by combining business and software engineering into a single, integrated discipline.

The Need for Business Engineering

As the competition for global markets heats up, the formula for gaining and holding market share is undergoing a major change. According to conventional marketing doctrine, a company should position itself along several critical dimensions, such as quality, time to market, and cost. A company that was the quality leader, for example, would not be expected to compete on the basis of price or time to market.

The requirements for success are changing

3

There is no room for compromise in the new competition. Companies are beginning to offer higher quality at lower prices, stealing market share from competitors that used to own either

Companies must now satisfy multiple demands

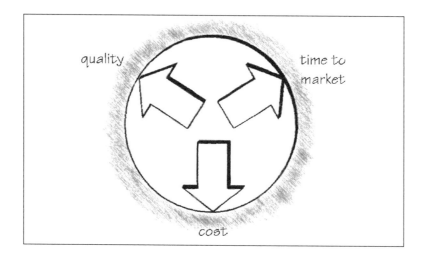

the "quality" or "low-cost" positions in their markets. And virtually every company is striving to bring new products to market
faster in order to meet increasingly volatile customer demands.
In short, the competitive edge now goes to companies that can
deliver better products faster and cheaper. Two out of three isn't
good enough.

**Better, faster,
and cheaper.**

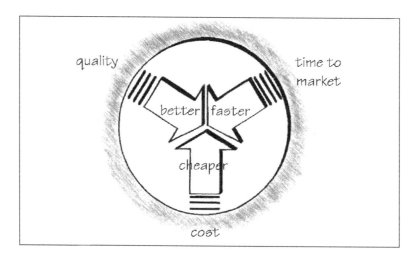

4

*Companies are
struggling to
survive*

This is a difficult challenge for any company. Yet it is the nature
of competition to continually up the ante of success, and the
emergence of global markets has rapidly driven competition to

unforeseen levels. If any company can bring better products to market with shorter lead times and reduced costs, others must follow suit or lose market share. Many companies now find themselves caught in a struggle for survival. The process of natural selection—which applies equally to organisms and organizations—ensures that only the fittest will survive.

Because companies have less room to differentiate themselves based on product positioning, they are left with only one option—to improve the operations that bring those products to market. To remain competitive, a company must view its processes in the same terms as its products and apply the same optimizations. Through the process of *business engineering*, it must improve the quality of its operations while reducing their time and costs.

Business engineering is the key to survival

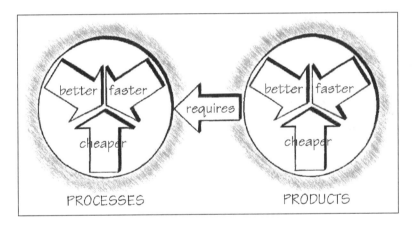

Competing through process.

The Quest for Continuous Improvement

Vital as it may be, there is a dark side to business engineering. Reinventing a company is painfully expensive in terms of cash, diversion of resources, disruption of operations, intellectual effort, and emotional trauma. The universal hope of these companies is that once their efforts are complete, they can take down the "Pardon Our Mess" sign and enjoy a new competitive position in their market.

Business engineering is expensive

One-shot solu-
tions are not
sufficient

Unfortunately, the results of business engineering are rarely this glorious. One of the harsh realities of business engineering is that it is not a one-shot effort. As companies throughout the world find better ways to streamline their businesses, there is a constant escalation of tactics and technologies. Moreover, the demands of consumers are constantly changing, requiring continuous realignment of resources to meet shifting buying patterns.

There is no sta-
ble formula for
success

Tom Peters, who has spent years attempting to isolate the critical factors that allow some companies to prosper while others fail, has come to the disturbing conclusion that there *is* no formula for success. The companies that win and hold market share in today's volatile market are the ones that actually relish the challenge of constantly changing business conditions.

Continuous
improvement is
essential

Thriving on chaos is a tall order. The constant escalation of demands on a company means that the competitive advantage resulting from reengineering a process may be highly transient. The only sustainable advantage comes from continuous optimization of processes, structure, and resource utilization.

Repeated engi-
neering doesn't
work

The demand for continuous optimization is often taken to mean that a company must undergo a relentless series of reengineering efforts, tearing out their current structures and processes and installing new ones so rapidly that the company is in a state of constant upheaval. Unfortunately, that turmoil inevitably reduces the quality of operations and may itself cause a decline in competitiveness. Anyone who has survived one or more organizational overhauls can attest to the confusion and paralysis these efforts create. Generating internal chaos is not the way to thrive on external chaos.

The ultimate
goal is
adaptivity

The operative word in the phrase "continuous optimization" is *continuous.* Continuity requires gradual rather than sudden change. This means that designing processes that are better, faster, and cheaper isn't really enough. These processes must also be designed to adapt to changing conditions gracefully while maintaining a competitive edge in quality, speed, and economy. Although designing in adaptivity is harder in the short term, it is easier in the long run because only a single overhaul is required. Once the adaptive systems are in place, individual operations can be continuously tuned to enhance their performance without creating disruptions or discontinuities.

The Role of Software Engineering

Modern organizations are critically dependent on their information systems for daily operations. Given this dependency, an essential aspect of any business engineering effort is the design of information systems that enhance the corporate process.

Information systems must be part of the solution

Although it may seem obvious that information systems must contribute to the improvement of corporate operations, a look at recent history suggests that this goal is an elusive one. During the 1980s, American companies spent in excess of a trillion dollars on information technology. During that same period, overall office productivity increased by only one percentage point. Given the obvious advantages of automating routine business processes, there is clearly something wrong with this picture.

They are currently part of the problem

Of course, this statistic is merely an average. Many companies have demonstrated significant increases in productivity from their investment in information technology. These companies do not contradict the overall statistic; they simply indicate that, as with all statistics, there is variation about the average. The existence of companies with significant productivity improvements actually suggests a more disturbing conclusion—that there must be a counterbalancing group of companies that have realized no gains at all or actually experienced decreased productivity as a result of their investment in information technology!

Some information systems do increase productivity

In an analysis of companies that have shown significant increases in productivity through the use of information technology, *Business Week* concluded that the key to achieving these benefits is coupling the use of technology directly to business engineering efforts. In each of the companies they examined, information technology helped increase productivity only when it was used to support new and better ways of conducting the business. Simply automating existing processes rarely improved productivity.

Benefits require coupling with business engineering

Although new information systems can increase corporate productivity if they are coupled with business engineering efforts, the requirement for continuous process optimization suggests that these benefits may be short-lived at best. With prevailing software development practices, it typically takes two to five years to bring new systems on line. During that time, business

The benefits of new systems may be short-lived

conditions may have changed dramatically. As the following illustration suggests, the resulting "solution" may fit the new business problem about as well as a square peg fits a round hole.

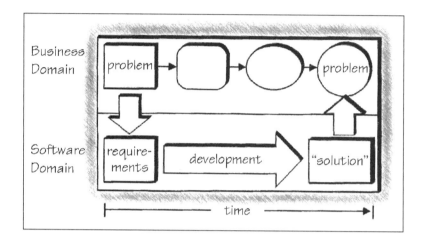

The demands for continuous process optimization require a radical rethinking of how information systems are designed and constructed. It is no longer sufficient to produce fixed solutions to fixed business problems. Information systems, like the business systems they support, must be adaptive in nature. They must be capable of sustained, graceful change in response to evolving business requirements, as shown below.

Adaptive information systems are essential

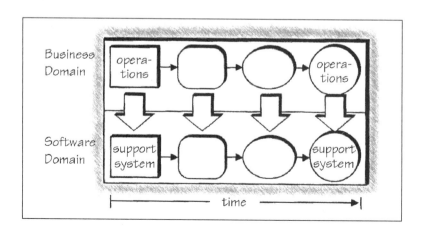

Convergent Engineering

In sum, sustained corporate competitiveness requires the engineering of adaptivity into both organizational processes and their supporting information systems. Each of these undertakings represents a major challenge. But combining the two represents an even more difficult problem. This is a case where the whole is much greater than the sum of its parts—both in terms of its value to the organization and the difficulty of its achievement.

Processes and systems must both be adaptive

Ignoring for the moment the requirement for adaptivity, simply combining business and software engineering is extremely difficult. The problem is that the two have historically been treated as very different endeavors. The two types of engineering involve different practitioners with different backgrounds using different techniques to achieve different goals. The inevitable result is radically divergent designs for the business and its software, as shown below.

Business and software systems are designed separately

Divergent models of business and software.

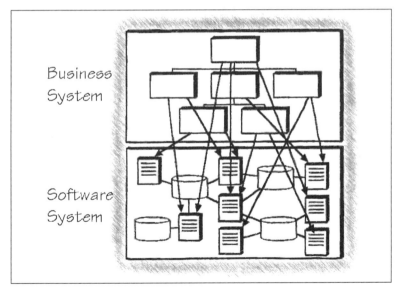

The conventional dichotomy between business and software engineering inevitably creates frustrating incompatibilities between the business and its software, with the two systems working in different ways toward different ends. The complexity that results from combining the two discrepant systems may

Divergent engineering leads to chaos

actually lead to chaotic organizational behavior, in the scientific sense of being inherently unpredictable and uncontrollable.

Divergent systems are resistant to change

Things become even more difficult when adaptivity is taken into account because the dichotomy between business design and software design makes the combined structure extremely resistant to change. Each half of the structure is already difficult to change: Organizations are notoriously rigid in the face of change, and conventional techniques of software development are designed to produce stable rather than flexible information systems. Combining the two halves multiplies the problem many times over. If a company makes even a modest change in the way it does business, it may have to make a large number of seemingly unrelated changes in its software systems to support that change, each of which is likely to disrupt other aspects of the business in unforeseen ways.

The result is organizational rigidity

The result is that most large companies are locked in place by their information systems. Even if they are able to change their business processes to adapt to changing circumstances, they are incapable of implementing those changes in their support systems without creating havoc with their ongoing business processes.

The solution is convergent engineering

The solution to this problem is to engineer the business and its supporting software as a single, integrated system. In *convergent engineering,* the business design is implemented directly in soft-

A convergent model.

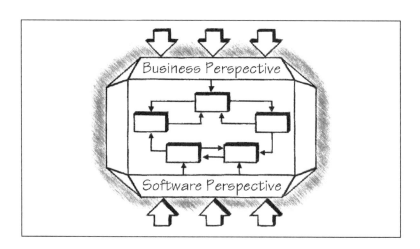

ware with an absolute minimum of translation or restatement. In effect, the two designs become two different facets of the same system, with the business demands serving as the driving force. This merging is the essence of convergent engineering.

Convergent engineering offers three major advantages over divergent approaches to engineering businesses and their information systems:

Convergent engineering offers three advantages

1. It *simplifies the engineering process* and reduces the total amount of work because there is only a single system to design and implement.

2. It *eliminates the gaps* between business processes and their supporting software, making both the business and its software easier to design and understand.

3. It *facilitates change* by minimizing the problem of coordinating modifications to the business and its software, making the adaptive organization a viable goal.

2

Model-Based
Business Systems

*The transition to convergent engineering requires a profound shift in the
thinking of both managers and technologists. Instead of managers posing
problems for technologists to solve by creating new applications, the two
groups must work together to create working software models of the
organization. These models provide a solid yet flexible structure on which
business solutions can be rapidly assembled. The result is that new ways
of doing business can be implemented in days or weeks rather than
months or years.*

The Collapse of the Software Silos

The essence of convergent engineering is designing a single system that represents both the business and its supporting software. In order to realize that objective, companies must take a
fresh look at the accepted goal of software development.

*The goal of soft-
ware develop-
ment must
change*

The process of developing software to support business processes is known as *application development.* The name of the process implicitly sets the goal of software development—to
develop programs, or *applications,* that apply information technology to the solution of specific business problems. As shown in
the following illustration, applications are generally monolithic in

*Business soft-
ware has
always been
application-
based*

13

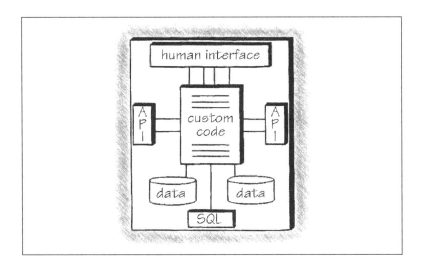

nature in the sense that each application can stand on its own, and each contains all the logic, functions, and information required to solve one particular problem.

Applications are designed by functional decomposition

Application programs have been the dominant form of business software since the inception of programming in the 1940s, and the procedures for developing applications are now well established. The primary design technique is *functional decomposition*. This process is based on breaking down the solution to a business problem into successively smaller units of functionality until a level is reached where the remaining tasks can be carried out by relatively short segments of instructions to the computer.

This produces a hierarchy of dedicated solutions

For example, solving a business problem might require solving three component problems, X, Y, and Z. Solving problem Y might require solving subordinate problems, A, B, and C. Solving B, in turn, might require solving problems 1, 2, and 3, and so on. In this approach, each component of a program is dedicated to solving a specific problem in the context of a larger, more general problem.

Applications are highly resistant to change

Functional decomposition assures that the detailed structure of a business solution is woven into the very fabric of an application. As a result, it is very difficult to change the solution without completely restructuring the application, a task which is usually more difficult than simply starting from scratch with a brand-new application. As for solving new business problems, it is virtually impossible to apply an existing application to a new problem because the design of applications is so problem-specific.

The application-based approach to software development arose during a period in which business problems were relatively stable and software was relatively simple. Under these conditions, a software solution could be developed fairly rapidly to address any given business problem, and the solution could be expected to remain valid for some years before being retired in favor of a new and better solution.

Applications require stability and simplicity

Neither of these conditions holds today. Business conditions are becoming increasingly volatile, and software is becoming ever more complex and difficult to develop. In most organizations, the so-called 18-month backlog—the delay before the development organization can begin work on a new application—is now up to about three years, and the time to complete new applications once they are started typically ranges from two to five years. The result of these two opposing trends—more rapidly changing problems and slower development of solutions—is that application development can no longer keep up with business problems.

Change and complexity are now the norm

15

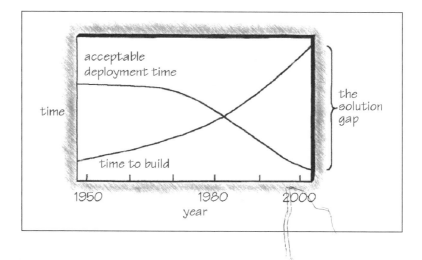

As a whole, the software industry has responded to this problem by seeking faster ways to develop applications. Fourth-generation languages, computer-aided software engineering (CASE) tools, object-oriented technology, and other techniques have all been developed to reduce development time. But accelerating the development process only forestalls the inevitable. The time has come when no reasonable degree of acceleration will allow the creation of new applications fast enough to meet changing business requirements. Monolithic applications—the software silos that populate the landscape of our information systems—are collapsing of their own weight, and building new silos faster is not the answer.

The Advent of Model-Based Systems

If building applications to solve business problems no longer works, what should the new strategy be? There is now a clear and compelling answer to this question: *model-based development.* The goal of this approach is to construct software models that represent the structure and operations of a business as simply and directly as possible. Because these models are not tied to any particular problem, they can be used to address a wide range of problems, including problems that weren't even imagined when the models were constructed.

The limitations of problem-specific applications are particularly evident in the manufacturing arena, which has now accumulated many different kinds of application software that are so resistant to integration they are referred to in the industry as "islands of automation." There are manufacturing resource planning (MRP II) systems, shop-floor control systems, inventory management systems, machine maintenance systems, personnel scheduling systems, accounting systems, and many more. The challenge is often portrayed as one of building bridges between these software "islands," but that would be only a partial solution at best. These systems were designed to stand alone, and they are never going to cooperate adequately to provide the integrated, adaptive software platform that modern manufacturing demands.

A far better solution is to construct a working model of a manufacturing company, including its organizations, processes, and resources. A model of a fabrication plant, for example, would contain software components representing the plant's work centers, inventory, work in progress, completed assemblies, personnel, and other key elements. At the top level, the model might look like the figure below.

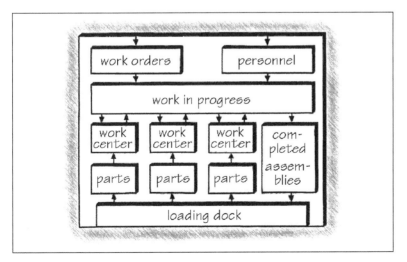

Modeling a fabrication plant.

Using the plant model

Once constructed, this model can be used to address the full range of business problems associated with managing the manufacturing process, as shown in the following illustration. Various techniques for addressing these problems can be tried, discarded, refined, and otherwise modified without necessarily reworking the fabrication model. Conversely, any change in the model, such as the addition of new kinds of machines or a restructuring of operations, is reflected simultaneously in all the business solutions.

Using the fabrication model.

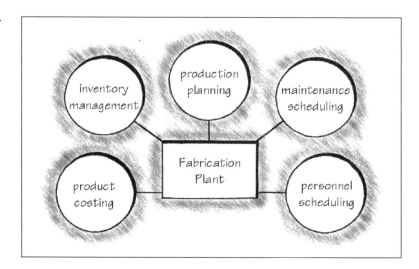

Models may be deeply nested

Modeling can take place on many levels. The model of the fabrication plant consists of many nested models. Each work center is a separate model, capable of addressing operational and scheduling problems on its own, independently of its larger context. Similarly, each machine within a work center is modeled as a self-managing resource, tracking its own maintenance and handling other activities that are specific to that individual machine. The division of labor among these lower-level models allows components to be added, removed, or replaced over time without redesigning the fabrication model as a whole.

Rapid order fulfillment

This nesting of models can be extended upward as well as downward. In the manufacturing example, models of fabrication plants, warehouses, supply chains, and administrative groups can be combined to form a model of the manufacturing department. This model can then be integrated into a higher-level model of

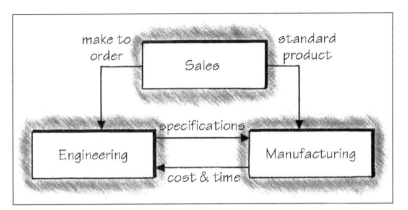

the order fulfillment process, as shown in the figure above. Each model manages its own affairs independently of the others, yet they all work together to solve higher-level business problems.

Because each model represents the operations and current state of a business entity, that model can be used to automatically estimate the time and cost to carry out a particular task. By connecting these models electronically, many activities that used to require human intervention can take place electronically orders of magnitude faster. In the manufacturing example, the time required for a salesperson to commit to a delivery date on a standard part that was out of stock but scheduled for production might be reduced from hours to seconds.

Models can reduce cycle times

Engineering and manufacturing could also communicate electronically during the design of a custom product, using the model of manufacturing—including its current workload, configuration, and staffing—to adapt a design to produce a quality product at the least cost and the shortest possible delivery time. This high-speed collaboration between engineering and design, known as *concurrent engineering* (not to be confused with convergent engineering), is a very desirable but highly elusive goal for manufacturing companies.

Concurrent engineering

19

The transition to model-based business systems will not be sudden, and existing applications—often termed *legacy systems*—will continue to play a crucial role for many years. Even the most avant-garde manufacturing company may want to stick with its existing machine-control systems, and it may be loath to touch

Models should leverage legacy systems

its mainframe-based accounting system. One of the goals of convergent engineering is to leverage these legacy systems while providing an easy migration path to model-based systems. Well-designed business models can do just that by accessing legacy systems transparently, allowing the functions of these systems to be incorporated into the model over time without disrupting corporate operations.

A layered architecture supports these goals

The software architecture that supports the model-based approach consists of horizontal layers rather than vertical applications. The models occupy the middle layer and form the integrating structure of the system. The top layer contains the screens and controls that let people use the models to run the business, while the bottom layer consists of all the legacy systems that execute operations not carried out within the model.

A layered architecture.

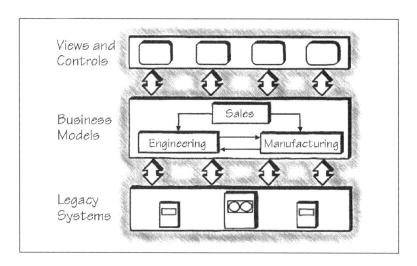

Combining Special-Purpose Models

Business modeling is a time-honored endeavor

Describing business systems in terms of models is complicated by the fact that the term *model* conjures up many different concepts. The software industry has offered up many different kinds of models in its first 50 years of existence, so there is no shortage of ideas to draw on when it comes to business modeling. In fact, the problem with modeling is not a shortage of models but an abundance of models which have almost no capability for productive interaction.

Consider the following five types of models:

There are many different kinds of models

❏ *Data models* are used to express patterns in the information that companies maintain about their customers, suppliers, products, and operations. Data modeling has been refined to a high art, with numerous methodologies and sophisticated notational schemes.

❏ *Process models* may be used to represent the flow of activity in certain business processes. Given the historical focus on developing problem-specific applications, however, most models of business processes are expressed only implicitly, in the flow of control within applications. More than one company has found itself sorting through millions of lines of COBOL code to rediscover its core business processes!

❏ *Work-flow models* are used to represent the sequence of human activities required to carry out business processes. These models are sometimes expressed in paper form only, as they are in most business engineering efforts. However, many are expressed directly in a new type of software, variously known as "work-flow software" or "groupware," that route documents and other information to people according to predetermined sequences.

❏ *Financial models* are used to project the consequences of various decisions and external influences on the financial status of organizations. These models may be expressed in sophisticated financial modeling systems, but they are most commonly found in spreadsheet models constructed by individual users.

❏ *Simulation models* are used to construct detailed representations of the entities and activities in an organization. These models provide insights into how the organization works and suggest ways to improve its functioning. Simulation models are most frequently found in process-intensive industries such as manufacturing.

21

These different types of models are all designed, constructed, maintained, and operated independently of each other. In most cases, the only two that actually reside in a company's mainstream information systems are the data and process models, and the task of coordinating these two models whenever one

All these models are constructed independently

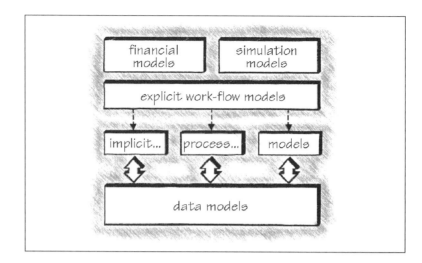

or the other changes is a continuing challenge for information-systems organizations. The other three models typically use dedicated, special-purpose software and have little or no contact with corporate information systems.

This dis-integrated approach doesn't work

This lack of integration severely restricts the value of the various types of business models. Budgets and sales forecasts generated in spreadsheets are usually collated manually, and they must be visually compared to actual accounting results in order to get any feedback on the accuracy of the projections. Similarly, enhanced procedures discovered through simulations must be programmed into all the affected applications and databases and then manually implemented as revised corporate operations. Modifications to business processes can sometimes be implemented directly in work-flow software, but only within the limitations of any applications that may be involved.

Convergent engineering requires integration

This practice of bolting models together through human labor can only be viewed as a transitional phase in the evolution of business modeling. The proper goal of business modeling should be to seamlessly integrate all these different aspects of a company into a single model that represents the company in a uniform manner. It is a fundamental tenet of convergent engineering that there is a single model of the company and its supporting systems. It follows that this unified model must embrace all the separate models that have been used to construct these supporting systems.

At the most basic level, it is critical to bring data and process together. In contemporary information systems, the greatest obstacle to change is not the restructuring of either applications or data, but the coordination of changes across these two domains. The only viable solution to this obstacle is to integrate data and process, repackaging them in ways that directly reflect the structure and operation of the organizations they support.

Data and process must be reunited

The model of the fabrication plant described previously must contain all the processes and data it needs to represent that plant in the functioning of the business as a whole. Within the model of the plant, each work center must contain all the processes and data it needs to function as an independent unit within the plant. In the nesting of models, process and data become tightly bound at every level.

Data in the fabrication plant

This merging of data and process can meet with some resistance from data management professionals because it appears to contradict the doctrine of *data independence.* In fact, just the opposite is true—the doctrine is not only satisfied, it is extended to include process as well as data. Simply put, the doctrine states that data should be stored in a manner independent of the way it is used so that new uses do not require restructuring. Merging data and process within conventional, monolithic applications would be a clear violation of this principle. By contrast, general-purpose models are designed to be independent of the uses to which they are put, giving them the stability and longevity that is sought through data independence. Preserving the independence of data as well as process is yet another reason for making the transition from conventional applications to model-based software.

Data independence is preserved

As to the other three models, it is vital that they be brought into the fold of real-time, operational systems. Financial projections should be calculated directly by the relevant business components and automatically compared with actual results. The capability for simulation should be fully integrated with operational systems so that enhancements discovered through simulation can be implemented with no additional programming. And choreographing the flow of work should be an integral part of all operational systems, not the result of an add-on program. In short, all of the different models in use today should become facets of a single, integrated business model.

The other models must become operational

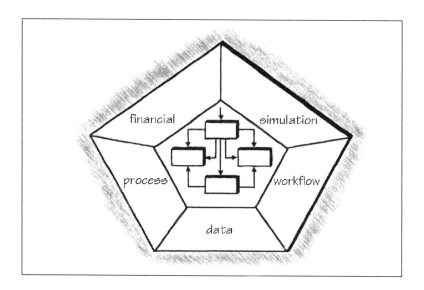

Integrated models serve three functions

A convergent business model gains considerable power by integrating the tasks of the five different models described earlier. Given this integration, convergent models can be used for three distinct purposes:

1. *Representation*—A convergent model represents the structure and process of an organization in a uniform way, making it easier to understand the company and to discover new ways to improve it.

2. *Simulation*—The same model can be used to make accurate projections regarding future operations, including resource requirements and cash flow. Simulation also provides a powerful tool for exploring the consequences of changes in business structures or processes in the pursuit of continuous optimization.

3. *Execution*—A convergent model is also the engine that powers the real-time execution of business operations. Using the model as an execution engine not only provides a higher level of automation, it also ensures that operations are actually performed in accordance with the model.

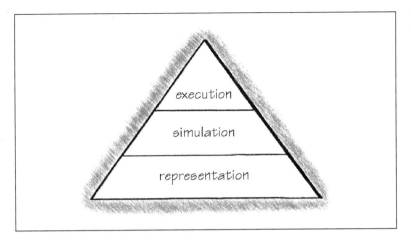

Managing Scale with Models

A long-standing problem that must be resolved in the new generation of integrated business modeling is the management of complexity. One of the "laws" of experimental psychology is that human beings cannot integrate more than seven to nine unrelated concepts. This limitation appears in every measurable aspect of human cognition, including visual perception, short-term memory, and cognitive analysis. Moreover, it has survived many hundreds of experimental tests conducted over a period of a hundred years, so there can be no question that the limitation is both real and pervasive.

Human comprehension is limited

Given this limited span of apprehension, what are we to make of data diagrams, process models, and other models that take up entire walls and require hours to trace and explain? The answer, unfortunately, is "not much." Our current modeling methodologies take no account of cognitive limitations. The result is an abundance of painstakingly crafted, highly detailed models that very few people can truly understand.

Business models are too complex

25

The difficulty in designing models that fall within the span of apprehension is that it's hard to build very interesting models without exceeding nine items. But the psychological research that demonstrates our limited comprehension span also reveals how we naturally work around this problem. The solution is a

The solution lies in chunking

mechanism called *chunking*. If people can work with a handful of items at a time and develop a firm grasp of how these items relate to each other, they can "chunk" the items together in their minds and use them as building blocks to construct a higher level of understanding. This process can be repeated to any degree of nesting as long as people have an opportunity to fully understand the pattern at each level.

Designing on a single plane

Consider the diagram below. It contains 81 items. This is not a particularly large number for a business design, but it's well beyond the span of apprehension. If this were a business model, most people would be hard pressed to understand how it worked, much less internalize it and use it as a mental model to guide their thinking and actions. The problem is that all 81 items are presented in a single plane, and all of them can interact directly with each other. Only a small fraction of the potential interactions are shown. There are 6,480 of them.

A flat design.

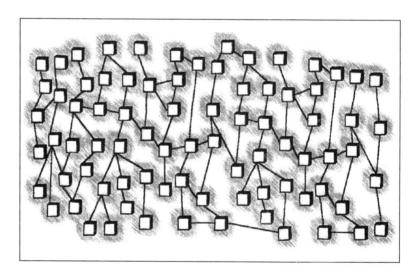

Designing in chunks

Now compare the next illustration. It contains the same 81 items, but they are chunked into groups of nine. Each group can be understood in isolation, then combined to form the whole. This is a pattern people can understand.

Chunking requires encapsulation

Chunking is more than just visual grouping. In order for the chunking technique to work, two conditions must be met. First, the items grouped together must form a meaningful pattern that

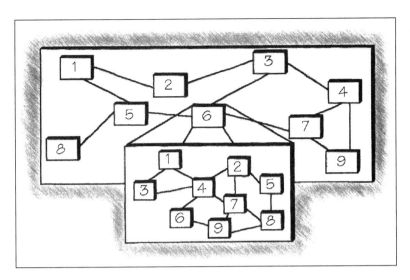

can be understood as a whole. Second, the items inside of a chunk can't interact directly with those of any other chunk. In programming terms, chunks must be *encapsulated*. If they aren't, then grouping items into chunks doesn't help because all the items still have to be dealt with at the same time.

The limited span of apprehension is well understood by software developers, who have been organizing large-scale systems into chunks called *modules* for many years. It is also implicitly understood by businesspeople, who have traditionally organized their companies into chunks called *business units, divisions, departments,* and other functional groupings. In keeping with the principles of chunking, each organization has a common theme or purpose which binds it together. Moreover, organizations are encapsulated in the sense that management activities follow a "chain of command" that prevents the direct interaction of thousands of people. Moreover, the number of components within each organization is typically limited to around seven to nine, which leads to multiple levels of nested organizations in larger companies.

Chunking is a natural technique

27

Despite the fact that both business and software professionals naturally apply the principles of chunking in organizing their daily work, analysts in both domains routinely produce wall-sized diagrams that are rendered inscrutable by their scale and

The basic rule is "nested nines"

complexity. It is time for all business models to be simplified through chunking, with no one model requiring the integration of more than seven to nine component models. Although nine is not a fixed limit—people can push the curve a little, especially if there are repeating items—it should be exceeded only under duress. By following the rule of nested nines, it is possible to build models with over 6,000 items using just four levels. Five levels bump that number to nearly 60,000, and six levels provide over half a million items. So it doesn't take many levels to build large systems using the rule of nested nines.

3

CHAPTER THREE

Building Models
with Objects

The early generations of computer languages were designed for communicating sequences of instructions to computers. Using these languages to replicate the complex, non-sequential interactions among the components of real-world businesses is an extremely difficult undertaking. By contrast, object technology was invented for modeling complex systems. With objects, it's actually easier to build models than to engage in conventional, sequential programming.

Object technology is the critical enabler for convergent engineering. The methodology is language-independent in that it does not depend on the features of any particular object language. But it does assume that objects provide the fundamental building blocks of all business models.

Object-Based Business Modeling

The advantages of model-based systems over conventional applications are sufficiently compelling that models will very likely prevail over applications regardless of the supporting technology. But conventional programming languages were designed for building conventional applications, and they are not well suited to modeling real-world systems. By contrast, modeling is precisely the task that object technology was developed to handle. The

Object technology was designed for modeling

original object-oriented language, SIMULA, is a simulation language for modeling the behavior of complex systems. All the successors to SIMULA, including the commercial object languages in use today, are ideally suited to building model-based systems.

Software objects represent real-world objects

The central activity of working with objects is not so much a matter of programming as it is *representation*. In object modeling, each important real-world object or concept is represented by a software object, and all the information and behavior associated with that real-world object are reflected in its corresponding software object. By faithfully representing the essential elements of a business in objects, it is possible to reproduce the behavior of that business by causing the objects to act out their roles within the model. The next illustration shows some of the many different kinds of objects that would appear in a typical business model.

Sample business objects.

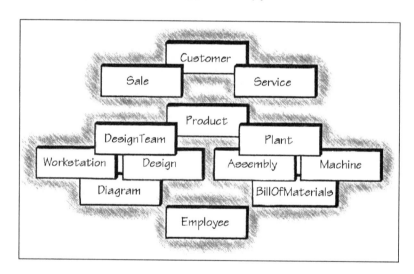

Objects are ideal for chunking

As described in Chapter 2, designing a large-scale model requires chunking related components into higher-level units. Objects provide an ideal implementation for chunks. First, they form naturally meaningful units because they are drawn directly from real-world objects in business. Second, they provide good encapsulation because they contain all the information they need to act appropriately in a larger context. Finally, objects support scalability because objects can be composed of other objects, allowing systems of any size to be constructed without violating the rule of nested nines.

Consider the fabrication plant described in Chapter 2. The plant itself is represented by a FabricationPlant object. That object is combined with objects representing other FabricationPlants, Warehouses, Suppliers, and AdministrativeGroups to form a model of Manufacturing as a whole. The Manufacturing object, in turn, is combined with objects representing other departments such as Sales and Engineering to form an object that represented a complete manufacturing company.

The fabrication plant

Chunking models with objects.

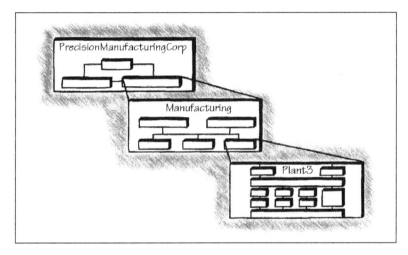

The FabricationPlant's internal structures are also modeled by objects. Part objects, once received at the LoadingDock, are held in Inventory until it is time to move them into WorkCenters. These WorkCenter objects contain Machines, Machinists, Subassemblies, and many other kinds of objects. Machine objects, in turn, are modeled to any level of detail using still lower-level objects. This nesting of objects continues until *base-level objects* are identified that contain no other objects. In this example, Date and MachineCycle might prove to be appropriate base-level objects.

FabricationPlant components

The quality that makes object technology such a powerful medium for business modeling is the direct mapping between models and objects. In convergent engineering, everything in the business is modeled by an object, and every object is a model of something in the business. A FabricationPlant object is a self-contained, working model of a real fabrication plant. A

Every object is a model

WorkCenter object is a model of a real work center, and a Machine object is a model of a real machine. This direct correspondence between objects and models continues right down to base-level objects and all the way up to the enterprise as a whole. The object is the sole and sufficient mechanism for both modeling the company and implementing models in software.

Base-level objects form the foundation

Elevating objects to the business level involves extending object concepts into a realm where they directly reflect the way managers view their companies. However, the basic concepts of object technology are the same regardless of the level, and these concepts must be understood in order for the extensions to make sense. The following sections provide a brief, language-independent introduction to object technology. This introduction was written for non-technical readers, and business relevance is favored over technical detail throughout. Readers who desire a more detailed explanation of objects should consult one of the books provided in the Suggested Readings.

Objects and Classes

Objects are defined by classes

Objects come in many different varieties, called *classes.* A class is simply a generic definition for similar objects, which are called *instances* of that class. Classes specify the kinds of things that their instance objects can know and do; for example, almost every business design requires a Customer class that defines the structure and behavior of Customer objects.

Objects have methods and variables

Objects contain methods and variables. *Methods* are named sequences of computer instructions that allow the object to carry out actions. They are the same as functions or procedures in conventional languages except that they are defined in the context of a specific class. *Variables* are named locations where data can be stored. They are the same as variables in conventional languages except that they can contain references to other objects in addition to such basic data types as numbers, dates, and text.

Classes define these methods and variables

The methods and variables contained in an object are defined by that object's class. For example, a Part class would define the methods and variables for all Part objects. Centralizing these definitions in classes avoids having to repeat them in every instance of that class. The following illustration demonstrates how a Part class would define the structure of Part objects.

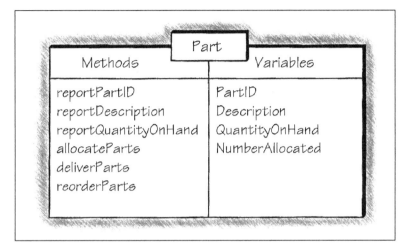

A Part class.

Given that a class defines the available methods and variables, all an instance of that class has to do is hold the values associated with its variables. Like any data, these values can change over time, either through interactions with other objects or through intervention on the part of a user.

Instances contain the values of variables

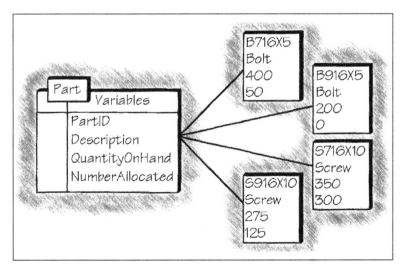

Instances of the Part class.

Objects, as defined by classes, are the fundamental building blocks for all object-oriented software. Constructing an object-oriented model consists of identifying the essential objects and then connecting them through object relationships. Three basic relationships provide the connections that bind objects together in meaningful patterns: (1) *specialization,* in which classes are defined as special cases of each other; (2) *collaboration,* in which objects send messages to each other to request services; and (3) *composition,* in which objects are constructed out of other objects. The next figure illustrates these three relationships, and the following sections examine each in turn.

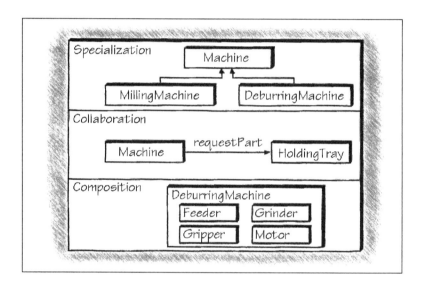

Relationship 1: Specialization

Although classes can be defined in isolation, they are typically defined as special cases, or *subclasses,* of each other. When a class is declared to be a subclass of another class, the new class automatically *inherits* all of the methods and variables defined in the existing class. Example: If the class SalesDepartment were declared to be a subclass of Department, then it would start with all the methods and variables defined in the Department class. New methods and variables could then be added to the SalesDepartment to give it the special abilities that made it unique.

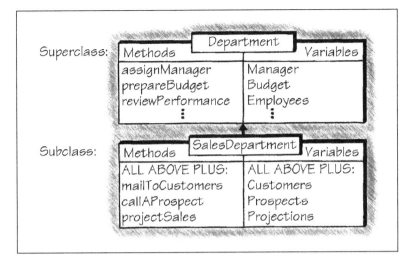

If the Department class had already inherited definitions from a higher-level class, or *superclass,* then the SalesDepartment would inherit those definitions as well. This inheritance mechanism can span any number of levels, allowing generic categories of objects to be refined to a high degree. The result of this layering of subclasses is a tree structure called a *class hierarchy.* The next illustration shows a small portion of a class hierarchy of business objects.

Subclassing can be nested

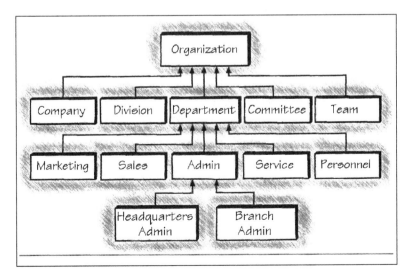

Part of a class hierarchy.

35

Classes look up the hierarchy

Note that the arrows shown in the class hierarchy point upward from a class to its superclass, not downward from a class to its subclass. This directionality is important. In order for inheritance to work, classes must know their superclasses. If a given class doesn't contain the definition of a required method or variable, it traces its way up the class hierarchy until it finds that definition. Consider the figure below. If the object representing the Seattle branch administrative department were asked to approve a budget, it would use the method defined by the company for all organizational units.

Looking up the hierarchy for a method.

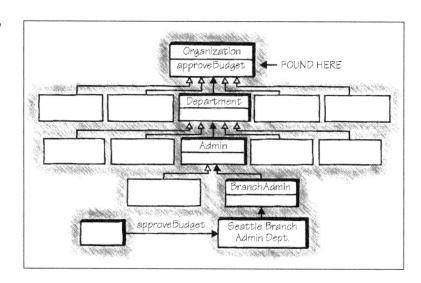

Overriding handles special cases

A useful by-product of this upward search is that local definitions override more general definitions. For example, all Product objects could share a common method for computing discounts, but some special cases of Product might use a different method. These special cases would be handled by defining a common *computeDiscount* method in the Product class, then placing more specific definitions of this method lower in the hierarchy. This technique, which is called *overriding,* ensures that the most specialized method available is always used because the upward search stops as soon as definition for the method is found. In the following figure, classes CP1000, CP2000, and CP3000 would use the special discounting method defined in CassettePlayer. All other products would use the generic method defined in the Product class.

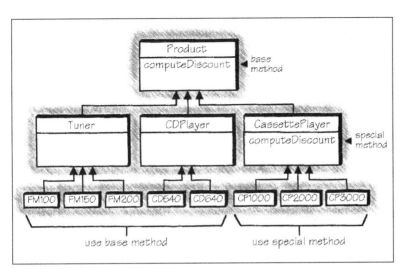

Relationship 2: Collaboration

Objects interact by providing services to each other. A *service* is simply a method within the object that can be invoked by other objects. For example, a Loan object might have a service called *calculatePayoff*. Any other object would invoke this service if it wanted to know the payoff amount of a particular Loan.

Objects provide services to other objects

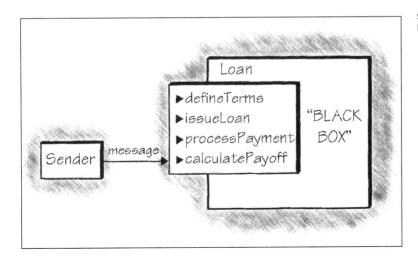

Services of a Loan object.

All access is through services

One of the fundamental principles of object technology is that the internals of an object—its variables and its non-service methods—are private to that object and may not be accessed or even examined from outside the object. In effect, an object is a "black box" component that reveals only the services it provides, which are collectively known as its *service interface*. This approach to building objects is not an innovation of object technology. It's simply a new application of the proven technique of *information hiding*, one of the basic tenets of good software design.

Information hiding facilitates change

Information hiding facilitates changes to objects by maintaining a clear distinction between the service interface of an object and its implementation. As long as the interface remains the same, the implementation can be modified without affecting any other object in a system. For example, the Loan object could be redesigned to change the way it decides whether to take a delinquent loan into collections. This redesign would not affect other objects in the model because no other object would know how the Loan made its decision in the first place.

Services are requested through messages

Objects request services from each other by sending *messages*. The message specifies the receiving object, names the desired service, and adds any specific values, or *parameters*, that may be required for the receiver to fulfill the request. The format of a message varies considerably among languages. The following message illustrates how a Loan might be informed of its basic terms:

Loan setTerms Principal:350,000 Rate:8.75 Term:180

Messages return a value

A message always returns a value to the object that sent it. This return value may be anything from a simple data value to a complex, nested object. At the very least, the receiving object will return some form of acknowledgment to the sending object that the message was received and processed. In the preceding example, the Loan object would return the software equivalent of "okay" to let the sender know that it had received and incorporated the new terms.

Messages can be nested

An object can respond to a message immediately, or it can send messages to one or more other objects in order to carry out the requested service. These other objects are often termed *collaborators* because they help the original object perform its task. The following figure shows a LoanEvaluation object requesting the

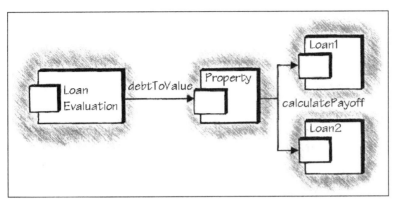

debt-to-value ratio of a Property that has a first and second mortgage on it. The Property calculates its current value, requests the two Loans to calculate their payoff amounts, accepts their answers, performs the required calculation, and returns the ratio to the LoanEvaluation object.

The way a message is handled is determined entirely by the object that receives it. This arrangement allows a single service to be carried out in many different ways, depending on the receiver. For example, a Department object could send the message *costFor: April* to each of its various components. Each component object would compute its cost in its own way, using the definition of the *costFor:* method found in its class. The following figure illustrates how differently this single message might be handled by different kinds of components.

Messages can be interpreted in many ways

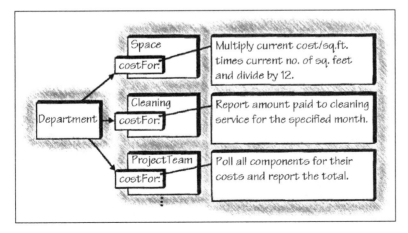

Costing components of a department.

39

The ability to use a single message to invoke many different kinds of behavior is known as *polymorphism.* The name may be awkward, but the mechanism is sheer elegance. It eliminates the need for tedious case statements, which would first identify the appropriate costing method and then call the corresponding function. More importantly, it removes business decisions from computer code. In the preceding example, new classes of objects could be added to Departments at any time. If these new objects required a different form of costing, then they would define their own *costFor:* method. The Department object would not have to be modified to handle these new types of components. In short, polymorphism simplifies the structure of business models while making them much easier to modify.

Relationship 3: Composition

Most business objects contain other objects. Such objects are known as *composite objects,* and the objects they contain are termed *component objects.* A composite object is created by placing references to component objects in its variables. Whenever a composite object needs to interact with its components, it looks up their current locations in the appropriate variables and sends them messages.

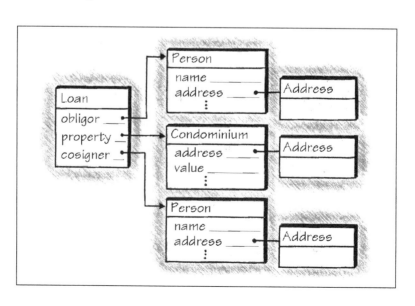

Because composite objects contain *references* to their component objects rather than containing the objects themselves, an object can appear as a component in any number of composite objects. A Customer could participate in any number of Purchases, a Product could appear in multiple SalesPackages, and an Employee could be a member of a Department, a HealthPlan, three Committees, and a ProjectTeam. As these examples illustrate, the ability to have objects be components of more than one composite object is critical to developing realistic business models.

Objects can appear in multiple composites

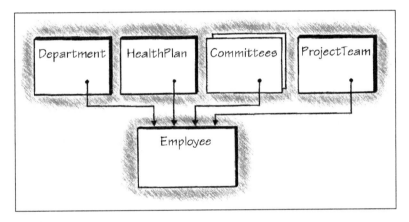

Employee object in multiple composites.

Even though composite objects are not physically contained inside of each other within the computer, it is often useful to think of them as being nested. Compare the two structures shown in the following figure. The first represents composition using org-chart notation, and the second uses graphic nesting. In general, representing composition as physical nesting in models is more compact and easier to understand at a glance.

Composition can be viewed as nesting

The objects contained in a composite object may themselves be composite objects, and these may contain other objects in turn. For example, a Division could contain multiple Departments, each of which could contain Equipment, Supply, Task, Employee, and other objects. Employee objects, in turn, could contain objects that represented prior positions, performance reviews, salary history, health claims, committee memberships, and other pertinent information. Deeply nested objects are com-

Composite objects may be nested

41

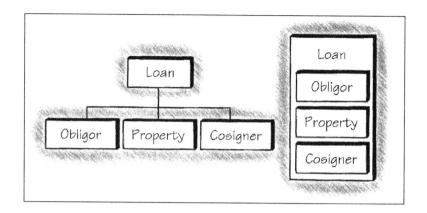

mon in business models, and they are very useful in bringing order out of complexity.

In order for this multilevel nesting to work effectively, each object should encapsulate its components as fully as possible. For example, a service department should provide an interface to other objects that hides its internal composition. If requests have to go to the components of this department, they should be received by the Department object itself and then passed on to the component. This is how companies usually operate, and the model should operate the same way for the same reason—it is the only way to avoid the explosion of complexity that would occur if all the elements of the business could interact directly with each other without regard for organizational structure.

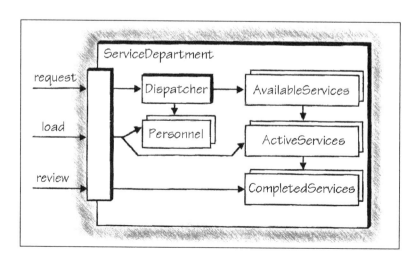

Fractal Composition

One of the most common themes in the structure of natural systems is *fractal patterns.* A fractal pattern is one that exhibits self-similarity at multiple levels. For example, the branching structure of a tree is a simple Y shape repeated at many levels, as shown in the following figure. The main trunk branches, each branch follows a similar pattern of branching, and so on, down to the level of the smallest twig. The same pattern of self-similarity at multiple levels can be seen in other natural systems ranging from the jagged form of mountain peaks to the whorls and swirls in smoke clouds.

Fractal patterns are common in nature

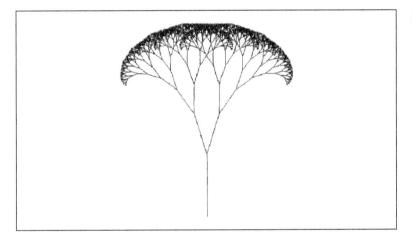

A fractal pattern in nature.

Fractal relationships can be used to considerable advantage in object-oriented design. A fractal object is a special type of composite object that contains instances of its own class as components. For example, a Product object could contain two or more component Products, each of which could contain Products in turn, and so on. This simple mechanism allows a single Product class to define an infinite variety of combination products, each with its own unique characteristics.

Fractals are a powerful design tool

Fractal objects allow object services to cascade down an entire complex structure with no additional programming. For example, a fractal Product object could combine the functions of a bill of materials and a bill of operations, determining all the material resources and manufacturing operations required to create the

Fractal products

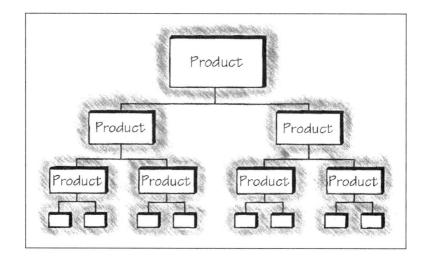

product. Similarly, any Product could cost itself, computing the
cost of its own materials and operations and then querying its
components for their costs. Each component Product would go
through the same procedure, cascading down the Product structure until the lowest-level components were reached, then
rolling the results back up the structure to the top-level Product.

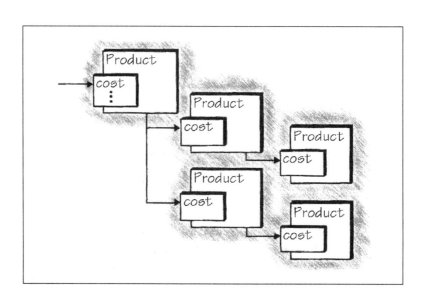

Managing Collections of Objects

There are many situations in business designs where multiple objects need to be managed together as a group. Object languages meet this requirement through the use of a special kind of composite object known as a *Collection* object. In every commercial object language, there is a predefined Collection class that is designed to contain groups of other objects. Collections offer standard services for adding, retrieving, and removing objects, and they can increase or decrease their size automatically based on the number of objects they are currently holding. This gives a business room to expand or contract without breaking its software or wasting computing resources.

Collections hold groups of objects

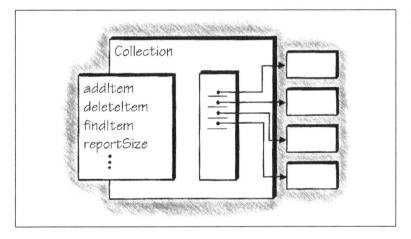

A Collection class.

In modeling a new kind of sales process, it may be essential for the Sales object to keep track of current prospects. The number of Prospect objects should start at zero and be able to rise to an arbitrarily large number depending on the success of the new sales process. The way to manage these Prospect objects is to create a collection to hold them, then place a reference to this collection in a variable named *Prospects.* Any method within the Sales object that needed access to Prospects would simply look in this variable and address its request to the indicated collection.

Tracking prospects

Because collections are used so commonly in business designs, it helps to use a special notation to denote a collection. A small icon representing a stack, as shown in the following figure, works

A special notation simplifies diagrams

45

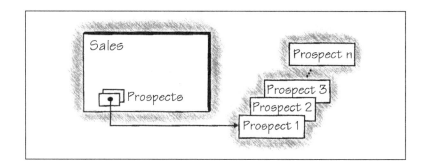

well because it immediately suggests more than one object. It is also helpful to name the collection using the plural form of the object it contains, using an adjective to indicate any restrictions on the collection. For example, the Products collection would contain references to all Product objects, whereas RecalledProducts would contain only Products that were currently subject to a recall.

Fractal objects rely heavily on collections

The fractal objects described in the preceding section usually have a variable number of fractal components. For example, a generic Organization object might consist of any number of component Organizations, each of which could have its own component Organizations, and so on. Although each Organization could be specified by an explicit variable, that would both complicate the design and reduce flexibility. It is much better to simply define an Organization object as having a collection of component Organizations. All component Organizations can then be addressed as a group, and the number and type of component Organizations is free to change at any time. As illustrated in the following figure, a single Organization class can be used to model the structure of an entire company in a simple, easily modified manner.

Polymorphism works well with collections

Collections are also helpful in leveraging the power of polymorphism. Consider the earlier example in which a department itemized the costs for all its components. The department would be allocated space, people, equipment, furniture, supplies, cash, and any number of other resources. Each resource would respond to the *costFor:* message in its own way. If all these resources were held in a collection, then all the required costs could be accumulated with a single message to the collection

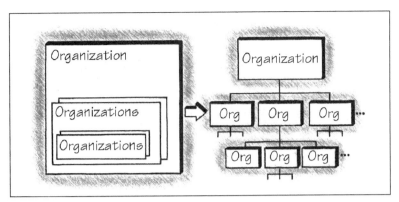

requesting it to ask each member for its *costFor:* service. This technique allows resources to be dynamically allocated to the department without requiring any change to the model.

Support for Convergent Engineering

One of the key advantages of object technology is that it naturally reflects the way people think. The real world consists of physical objects that we represent internally by forming *mental models* of those objects. As we build up our understanding of the world around us, we use many of the same relationships employed by object technology. Cars and houses contain many component objects that interact with each other in predictable ways. Moreover, there are many different kinds of cars and houses, such as sports cars and mansions, that are distinguished by special characteristics.

Object technology mirrors human thinking

The inheritance mechanism used in specialization maps particularly well to the way we naturally categorize real-world objects. In a process known as *generalization,* we learn to identify characteristics that group related things together. In *specialization* we learn to identify characteristics that signal important distinctions among things that are similar but different. And we make extensive use of overriding, using general rules for general cases and then memorizing specific exceptions to these rules. In general, birds can fly. But don't mention that to a penguin.

Inheritance mimics generalization

47

Objects facilitate modeling

The fact that object technology reflects these fundamental cognitive processes is one of the reasons it is the critical enabler for convergent engineering. It is much easier to map a mental model of a business into software when the software directly supports the way managers think about their businesses. This direct mapping eliminates the need for separate models to represent the way the business is viewed and the way its support systems are designed. Given the naturalness of object technology, a single model can serve both purposes without compromising either.

Objects help integrate models

Object technology also provides an excellent vehicle for combining the various types of business models discussed in Chapter 2. Each of the five types of business models can be expressed as a different facet of a unified object model:

❏ *Data* and *process models* are fully integrated because each object contains all the information and processes it needs to play its role in a larger context. Again, a well-designed object actually hides the distinction between data and process, allowing transparent migration between the two. If a loan object is asked to report its payoff amount, it is completely up to the loan object whether it retrieves this amount from a variable or calculates the amount on the fly.

❏ *Financial models* can be integrated directly into object-based business models. The key technique is to allow objects to manage their own financial affairs, requesting budget allocations, reporting expenditures, projecting revenues, and so on. Building financial management directly into operational systems offers the potential for real-time financial controls, and it supports the use of actual rather than average costing for products and services.

❏ *Simulation models* can also be implemented within an object model of a business. To use an object model as a simulator, make a copy of a model, including all its current information, and run various scenarios using hypothetical inputs. This technique allows managers to play "what if" not with a spreadsheet of numbers but with their entire company. If they discover changes to the model that promise to enhance operations, they can roll those changes over into the operational version.

❑ *Work-flow models* can also be realized in object models. As objects carry out their responsibilities within the business model, they naturally call upon both people and other objects to perform required tasks. Unlike conventional work-flow software, these interactions are fully encapsulated within each object, making them easy to modify and enhance over time.

PART TWO

Application

4

Preparing for a
Design Session

The second section of this book focuses on the actual practice of convergent engineering, illustrating the process with a hypothetical distribution company that deals in computers and electronic components. Dylan Distributors wants to improve its core operations to reduce costs and shorten customer response time. The next three chapters will show how the Dylan design team prepares for their business design session, conducts the session itself, and then details the resulting model to prepare it for implementation. The example is highly simplified to accommodate space constraints, but it should suffice to give you a sense of convergent engineering in action.

Recruiting the Team

The first step in designing a business model is to put the right people on the project. The members of the team should include business experts in the domain to be modeled, trained object modelers, a facilitator, and a scribe. It's best if the team is small—preferably 10 or fewer—because larger groups tend to lose focus and have greater difficulty carrying out the tasks required of them. It's also important to get an equal mixture of business experts and object modelers to maintain the proper balance in the convergent engineering process.

Keep the team small and balanced

53

A team assembled at a table.

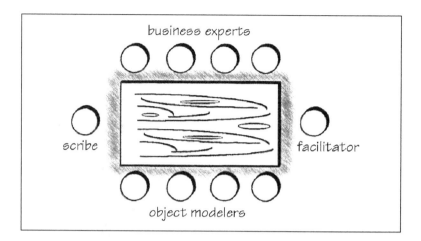

Recruit and motivate the best experts

The rank or position of the business experts is not important. They may be senior managers, clerical staff, factory supervisors, or any combination of these roles. The important thing is that they truly understand the business process being engineered and that they are sufficiently creative to develop new ideas about how that process can be improved. It is also essential that they be motivated to participate in the process. Nothing will kill a design more quickly than business experts who, like weary blood donors, have given knowledge one too many times. If the business members have already been involved in previous design activities, it is important to explain to them how this one is different and to be certain of their enthusiastic participation before bringing them into the team.

Use trained object modelers

The technical members of the team should be well versed in the theory and practice of object-oriented design. They should also be skilled in the use of two or more object languages so that they can think about objects in a language-independent way. If object modelers with this background are not available, the best qualified candidates should be given at least two days of intensive design training and two weeks of language training in a "pure" object language such as SmallTalk. This investment in training object modelers is one that will repay itself many times over in measurable business benefits.

Use a professional facilitator

An experienced facilitator is also essential to a successful design session. The facilitator must have well-developed skills in facilitating group processes, must be experienced in business engineering, and should be highly familiar with object modeling. This is an unusual combination of skills, and you may have to go outside the company to find a good facilitator or send qualified candidates out for special training. Of the three skill sets, the facilitation skills are the most vital. Although object modeling skills are essential, the mastery of these skills does not automatically make someone a good facilitator for the convergent engineering process.

It is also important to designate one person to serve as a scribe for the session. This person is responsible for capturing information generated during the design discussions and making sure it is accurately reflected in the model. This frees up the other team members to generate and to explore ideas without having to worry about recording them along the way. Although relatively passive during the design process, the scribe must be trained in the techniques of object modeling in order to capture the right information in a useful form.

Have a scribe capture ideas

Many companies want to involve additional people in the design process as observers so that they can learn from the process. Experience indicates that this is not a good idea. Having observers in the room creates a level of self-consciousness that interferes with creativity. Moreover, requiring a knowledgeable human being to remain mute while watching other people engage in an exciting, creative process is an act of cruelty. Even the most resolute observer will have leapt into the fray or headed for the door by the end of the first day.

Exclude observers

Dylan Distributors wants to focus its first effort on its purchasing, inventory, and sales operations. The team leader is Bill Johnson, COO, the internal champion for applying objects to business engineering. The other business members of the team are Marty Klein, a purchasing agent; Carol Williams, the company's inventory control manager; and Jean Sutherland, a sales manager. These business members are complemented by four object modelers, all of whom have been trained in convergent engineering but have no real-world experience with the process. A facilitator and scribe have been retained from an outside firm.

Team composition

Ignoring seniority and position in picking his team, Bill Johnson went for the best people he could get. Marty Klein has been with the company for 13 years and can work deals no other pur-

Selection criteria

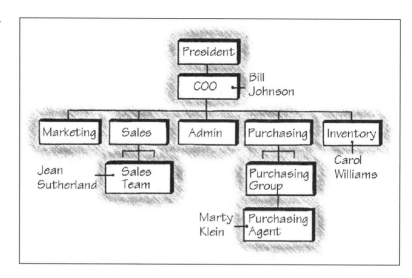

chasing agent can match. Carol Williams, new to the company, has been brought in to help reduce the escalating costs of inventory. Jean Sutherland has the most effective sales team in the company, but she has been complaining about Dylan's antiquated sales system and is pushing for a new approach. In recruiting the team, Bill assured each member that they would be able to criticize current operations freely and argue for improvements with no repercussions from management. He has promised them that if they can design a better system that can be built at a reasonable cost, it *will* be constructed and given a fair trial regardless of any objections that might arise.

Preparing for the Session

Take the session off site

It's a good idea to take the team off site and focus its attention exclusively on the design process. To achieve this end, you must provide relief for managers who are serving as business experts. Otherwise, they will tend to disappear from the design room and run their operations by telephone. An off-site session also puts managers more at ease in casual attire, which helps increase creativity and facilitate open communication among people at different levels within the company.

The physical space in which the design work is conducted is an important consideration. The first ingredient is a table just large enough to comfortably seat the 10 or so people on the team. The design will be created on this table, so it must be small enough that people can actually work at it but large enough that everyone has comfortable access. The size of the room is also important—it should be considerably larger than the table so that people can easily move around it, and there should be an open space at one end where the team can do role playing away from the table. Another critical ingredient is an abundant supply of writing surfaces and colored markers. Much of the design process involves informal sketches and notes that the team must be able to view as a group.

Create a good space

Of course, there is a limit to how long a team can maintain its intensity and focus, and business experts are particularly sensitive to time away from their regular responsibilities. Setting the duration of the design effort in advance not only allows participants to manage their schedules, it also puts a hard deadline on the deliverable that motivates a sustained effort. Experience suggests that a week is a good amount of time for a business design effort. It's hard to accomplish much in less than five days, and it's difficult to keep the energy level up much longer than that.

Set a reasonable duration

Once the design team has been recruited, it should meet one or more times to let people get to know one another, gain consensus on the goals of the project, and discuss the agenda for the convergent engineering session. If the team is being recruited from remote locations and can't be assembled in advance, the following activities can be merged into the week-long design session. However, reflection and the passage of time can be quite useful in grappling with the issues raised in these preliminary discussions, so it is generally more effective to get the team together at least twice before the design week.

Activate the team

Bill Johnson has just called his team together for the first time. He has already held a series of informal meetings with selected business experts to firm up the composition of the team and get buy-in for the convergent engineering approach. The current meeting is a half-day session involving the entire team, including its newly trained object modelers. The purpose of the meeting is to discuss the scope of the model that is to be constructed and gain consensus on the goals of the project.

The first meetings

57

Establishing the Domain

Start by setting the boundaries

Before modeling can begin, the team must agree on the bounds of the model. There are many techniques for performing a domain analysis, but a simple approach generally proves adequate. The facilitator draws a large blob on a chart or a whiteboard to represent the domain to be modeled, then has the team members name organizational units or processes that lie inside or outside the domain, as shown below. It's best not to analyze each component as it is named but simply enter its name inside or outside the blob, as appropriate. If members of the team question the placement of an element, put a question mark next to it and go on to the next element.

A basic domain diagram.

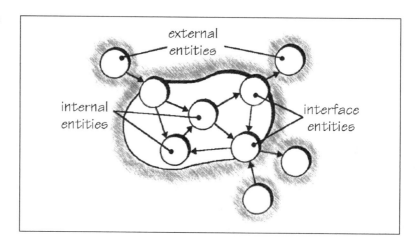

Arrange components by interaction

When the team runs out of design elements or starts suggesting elements that seem too low-level for a first-cut analysis, take some time to examine the diagram and look for patterns. If necessary, rearrange the components so that components that interact are adjacent to one another. Similarly, components outside the domain should be drawn close to any components inside the domain with which they interact. The spans between these two begin to suggest where the model will need interfaces to external systems. Components inside the domain that can communicate with external components should be shown penetrating the boundary of the blob.

After several passes, the Dylan team comes up with the domain diagram shown below. Carol Williams points out that although customers and suppliers are shown outside the domain of the project, they will have to be represented in the model somehow if the model is to work. The facilitator explains that placing external entities outside the boundary means only that the model is not responsible for the actions of the actual, real-world customers and suppliers. Customers and suppliers will still be included in the model, and the objects that represent them will actually serve as their electronic agents within the model. With that understanding, the team agrees on the analysis as a reasonable starting point.

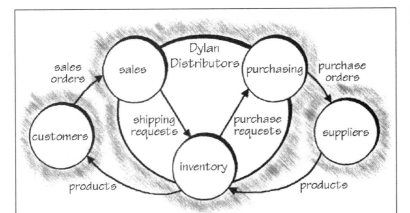

Handling Large Domains

One of the most common reactions to the initial domain analysis is that the project is much larger than originally envisioned. This may not be a problem—it is possible to develop high-level models of considerable breadth very rapidly using the techniques described in this book. However, if the scope truly does appear to be much larger than the team can handle in a week, then a decision must be made to limit either the depth or the breadth of the effort.

The domain may be too large for one session

59

The choice between breadth and depth is an important one because it determines the kind of model the team will generate. If the team chooses to go for breadth, then it will produce a

Choosing breadth creates a shallow system

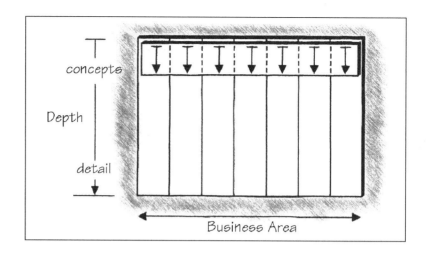

broadly applicable model that defines the key business objects
that appear throughout the domain. However, the model will be
too shallow to extend down to the detail level, so the design
effort won't yield a blueprint for a working system.

*Choosing depth
produces a
narrow system*

By contrast, a choice for depth means focusing on a vertical slice
of the domain and leaving other aspects of the domain for future
sessions. A depth-first approach should yield a design with sufficient detail to guide the construction of a working system, but it
runs the risk of defining business objects in a narrow sense that
does not generalize well to other areas of the domain.

**A narrow, deep
model.**

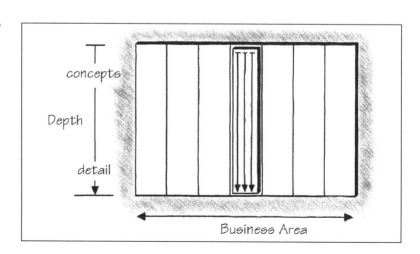

An obvious option when faced with a large domain is to break the modeling effort into multiple sessions. But choosing this option still begs the question of depth versus breadth. The best resolution to this dilemma is a combination strategy called the *T Technique*. In this approach, the initial design session tackles the entire domain and attempts to characterize the key business objects as generically as possible. This first session is also used to identify the most opportune areas for in-depth design. As the second and subsequent sessions drive the model down into greater levels of detail within the selected areas, discoveries at the deeper level are fed back up to the broad model. In this way, the high-level model serves as an overall guide for modeling each area, yet continues to evolve and adjust as each area is modeled in detail.

The best solution is breadth, then depth

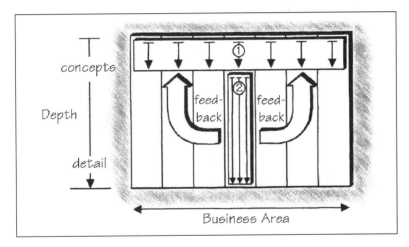

The T Technique.

Defining Business Scenarios

Once the team has agreed on the domain of the model, it needs to identify the most critical operations the model will carry out. The most common way to formalize these requirements is to generate operational scenarios—often referred to as *use cases*—that correspond to key business processes. These scenarios are defined prior to developing the model, then used throughout the design process to test the correctness and completeness of the design. Some tools and techniques for formalizing these scenarios are described in the Suggested Readings.

Scenarios script critical operations

The Dylan team considers a variety of different business scenarios, but they keep coming back to two core activities—selling products to customers and purchasing products from suppliers. The team decides to design the model around these two primary scenarios. It will then consider a range of variations on each basic scenario to make sure that any exceptions can be handled. The team will "execute" the two basic scenarios throughout the design week, rolling in the variations toward the end of the week to complete the validation of its design.

The first scenario models the simplest of sales, in which a customer calls in and places an order for products that are in inventory. The sequence of activities is as follows:

1. Customer calls in and is routed to the assigned salesperson.

2. Customer agrees to buy several products in various quantities.

3. An inventory check reveals that the products are on hand.

4. A sales order is generated, printed, and mailed to customer.

5. The products are shipped from the warehouse.

The second scenario captures the basic process by which products are reordered. This scenario is not quite as clear to the team because it plans to focus a great deal of attention on the problem of inventory management and optimal reordering. For the time being, it expresses the scenario as follows:

1. A product falls below its optimal inventory level.

2. A purchase order is generated automatically to reorder the product.

3. Potential suppliers are selected based on price, quality, and delivery.

4. The purchase order is sent to the supplier.

5. The ordered products are received and placed in the warehouse.

In addition to these two basic scenarios, the design team has a wish list of capabilities it would like to realize within the model. In simplified form, it reads as follows:

1. Discounts can be applied to any product or customer. Discounts can be graduated according to the number of products ordered, the dollar amount of any order, or the total sales to a customer over any specified period. Any comparable discounts on the purchasing side should also be modeled and factored into buying decisions.

2. The model actively assists in the collection of receivables, analyzing each customer's normal payment cycle and responding to any deviations with collection letters and more aggressive actions as needed. The credit standing of any customer is immediately available to salespeople so that a customer can be shifted to a cash-only basis if appropriate.

3. The model analyzes sales patterns for every product over every customer, generating statistical predictions of future sales. These projections are used in both managing cash flow and optimizing stock on hand. The model actively seeks to maximize inventory turns and minimize carrying costs while keeping backorders to an acceptable level.

4. The model provides actual costing of all products, including the cost of carrying each individual product in inventory, and automatically computes profit margins for every transaction.

5. The model provides extensive on-screen assistance in responding to customer requests, generating sales orders, and preparing purchase orders. It also provides graphic feedback on sales and purchasing activities.

6. The model handles such routine administrative tasks as recording transactions with customers and suppliers, keeping online catalogs of products and prices for each supplier, as well as adding and removing customers, suppliers, salespeople, and purchasing agents.

Evaluating Legacy Systems

Legacy systems must be incorporated

Most methodologies for designing object-oriented systems tend to ignore the issue of existing, conventional systems, implicitly assuming that each business design starts with a clean sheet of paper. Real companies rarely have this luxury. They can't ignore the millions of dollars they have invested in their existing information systems, nor do they want to take their company through the trauma of an overnight conversion to a new technology. Any object-oriented solution they adopt must include a way to make effective use of these legacy systems, at least as a transitional strategy.

Legacy systems can't dictate the design

At the same time, there is a real danger in focusing too heavily on the capabilities and limitations of existing systems when designing an object-oriented business model. If a business model is molded around existing systems, it can easily take on the shape of those systems. This is bound to distort the model and leave a permanent impression that may be hard to eradicate as legacy systems are taken out of service.

Start with an inventory of existing systems

A good compromise strategy is to take an inventory of the relevant existing systems prior to the business design session. This inventory should summarize the key technical characteristics of each system, including its basic capabilities, platforms, number of users, usage rate, volume of data, format and accessibility of data, degree of dependence on other systems, and the availability of interfaces for controlling the system with other programs. The inventory should also rate each system in terms of how well it is serving the needs of the business and how easily it can be modified to meet changing needs.

System inventory

The Dylan design team identifies five existing systems that affect operations within their domain. Chief among these is a 10-year-old accounting system running on a mainframe. It includes modules for Purchasing, Sales, and Inventory Management. The purchasing and sales departments use the first two modules for cutting purchase orders and entering sales orders, respectively. The Inventory Management module doesn't allow a sufficient breakdown of products for Dylan's needs, so the purchasing department has a separate Product Control System running under UNIX that tracks inventory more precisely and feeds summary data to the accounting system. A Warehouse Control

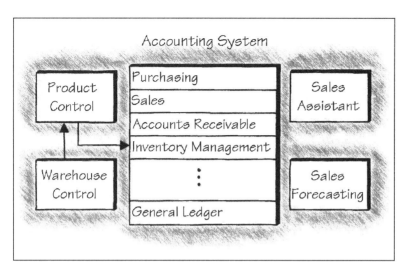

System running on a minicomputer manages physical product handling while also keeping the Product Control System up to date. On the sales side, the company does sales forecasting on PC-based spreadsheets, and Jean Sutherland's group has put together a Sales Assistant application in Visual BASIC that has proved quite useful but suffers from its stand-alone status.

Once this inventory has been completed, the existing systems should be evaluated in terms of priority for replacement. Large, expensive systems that are working well and are easy to access by surrounding systems are excellent candidates for incorporation into the next-generation business platform. Small, closed systems that are no longer serving the needs of the business are good candidates for early replacement. Systems that fall between these two extremes require careful judgment calls.

Prioritize these systems for replacement

The Dylan team doesn't want to touch the accounting system despite its known weaknesses because the costs of conversion would almost certainly outweigh the benefits. The Warehouse system, although running on an aging platform, is doing its job well enough and is open to outside access. But the Product Control System has become a hopeless kludge and is definitely due for replacement. Jean Sutherland is adamant that sales forecasting be removed from spreadsheets and brought into the object system, and she would like to toss her Sales Assistant

System evaluation

65

application and roll its functionality into the object model as well. Given her vehemence, no one dares voice any objections. The result: A preliminary decision is made to leave accounting and warehouse control alone, but to replace the Product Control System, the Sales Assistant, and the spreadsheet-based sales forecasting process.

Ignore existing systems in designing the model

Once the evaluation of existing systems has been completed, it should be set aside and ignored during the basic design process. This is critical for building a good object-oriented model that can support both the current way of doing business and the enhanced business processes that are developed during the design session. Design the ideal system first, then figure out how to make use of legacy systems. The reason for evaluating legacy systems in advance of the design session is not to shape the design, but to help the team focus its efforts on the areas where its model will add the most value.

5

CHAPTER FIVE

A Convergent
Engineering Session

It's time to build the model. Although the experience of the Dylan team should give you some sense of what transpires in an actual design session, it's hard to communicate the intensity of the drama that often unfolds. If done well, the session can have a transforming effect on the participants as well as the company. However, there's no fixed recipe for leading people into breakthrough thinking, and every session follows its own path to success. My recommendations are simple: Think boldly, argue cleanly, and have fun. You will know when you are making progress when you suddenly stop shouting long enough to realize that you are in violent agreement.

Starting the Session

The first order of business is to let people know how the sessions will be conducted and what their roles will be. Given that business design is a highly exploratory activity, a fixed agenda for each day of the week is not feasible. However, an overview of the basic progression is helpful for setting expectations. The following table summarizes this progression. If some of the tasks described in Chapter 4 have not been completed, these will have to be inserted at the front of the design session, reducing the amount of design work that can be accomplished during the week.

Establish the agenda

67

	AM	PM
Monday	Explore objects	Sketch model
Tuesday	Assign responsibilities	Define relationships
Wednesday	Talk through	Extend model
Thursday	Walk through	"Break" model
Friday	Run through	Optimize model

Set appropriate expectations

It is important to set expectations for the session that are ambitious yet realistic. The goal is to design a flexible, extensible model of the business domain that can execute core business processes as efficiently and effectively as possible. The model will be expressed in terms of objects, but these objects will be defined only at the business level. Detailing of the objects will be carried out by the object modelers at the conclusion of the design session.

Discourage technical discussions

The key to designing a solid business model in the span of a week is to avoid getting bogged down in detail. The team should continually strive to model the chosen domain to an even depth and avoid plunging deeply into any one area. It is particularly important to postpone any discussion of implementation issues. One of the strengths of convergent engineering is that it is language-independent, so that discussions of particular object languages are irrelevant in these meetings. Similarly, the group should simply assume that all objects are inherently persistent, without worrying about whether they will be stored in an object database or in some other format.

Prepare for constructive conflict

It is also important to prepare team members for the disagreements that will inevitably occur and to provide them with some psychological tools for managing these disagreements. One useful ground rule is that everyone is equal on the team, regardless of his or her rank within the company. Another rule is that only one person speaks at a time so that team discussions don't degenerate into separate, private arguments. It is up to the facilitator to set the rules, get buy-in from the group for these rules, and gently enforce them throughout the week.

Sketching the Initial Model

The first step in building the business model is to look for the objects that are most essential to carrying out the primary business scenarios. Start out as simply as possible, designing a minimal model that spans the domain. Then gradually extend the model by refining the definition of your initial objects and adding new objects as required.

Start by looking for generic objects

As you consider candidate objects and their possible relationships, draw some informal sketches on the whiteboard. Use simple rectangles to represent objects and apply the "stack" notation for collections as these become apparent. Throw in some arrows wherever you think objects may need to interact through messages, and nest objects inside of other objects if you think they will turn out to be components. Don't worry about representing specialization at this point—it isn't particularly useful in the initial stages of modeling, and including it in the same diagram as composition and collaboration tends to make the diagrams confusing.

Begin with simple sketches

The Dylan team builds its initial model around its two basic business scenarios—selling products to customers and purchasing products from suppliers. It decides to sketch these processes as two basic cycles, side by side, with inventory as the point of intersection. Their first diagram is shown in the following figure.

First model

Identifying Classes

Once you have a sketch you like, you should start transforming the shapes in your diagram into descriptions of working objects. The mechanism for doing this is a specially formatted index card known as a *class card*. Class cards have sections for capturing critical information about the class and its relationships to other classes.

Capture objects on class cards

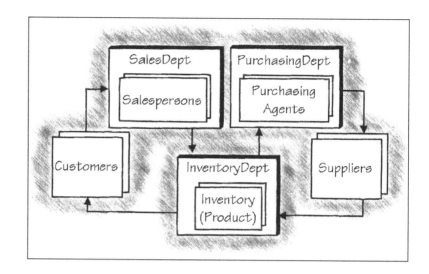

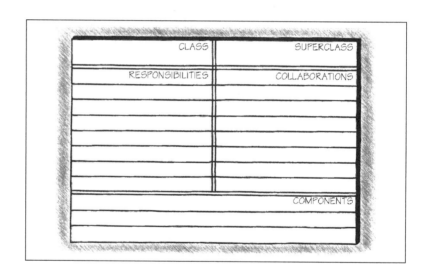

70

Start by choosing a name

The only thing you need to enter on a class card when you first define it is its name. This is a small but important step because the name you give each class will have a significant effect on the ease with which businesspeople grasp the workings of the model. The name you choose should communicate clearly and succinctly, in business rather than technical terms, what each type of object represents in the real world.

The Dylan team identifies eight classes from their initial sketch: Product, Customer, Supplier, Salesperson, PurchasingAgent, and three departments—Sales, Inventory, and Purchasing. The team creates cards for their initial classes and lays them out on the table according to their diagram, as shown below. In the case of the composite department classes, the cards are cascaded to reflect the nesting in the diagram.

Initial classes

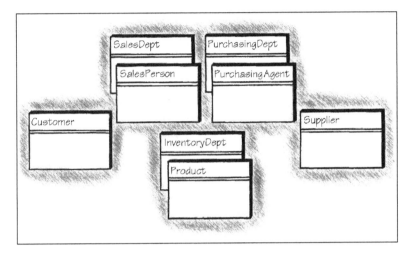

Initial card layout.

Once an initial set of classes has been identified, it's time to review those classes and start adding detail. At this point, the design process has reached a critical juncture. Many popular object-oriented design methodologies portray objects as being "data-centric" and encourage modelers to define classes in terms of the variables they contain. In support of this approach, most "object-oriented" computer-aided software engineering (CASE) tools provide extensive facilities for defining variables, and they will automatically generate corresponding "get" and "set" methods for accessing these variables.

Don't define classes by their data

This approach is questionable on two counts. First, it encourages the generation of passive objects that do little more than manage packets of related data. More importantly, it violates encapsulation by publicizing information that should be private to the object. Violating encapsulation makes it much more difficult to modify object models because it creates complex dependencies among the objects.

The data-centric view violates encapsulation

Defining Responsibilities

Responsibilities respect encapsulation

The primary alternative to defining objects in terms of their data is to define them according to the roles they play in the model. This is the essence of a technique known as *responsibility-driven design*. In this approach, each object is viewed as an active entity within the model, carrying out specific responsibilities in order to fulfill its role. It is up to the object—as defined by its class—how it uses variables in carrying out those responsibilities.

Define responsibilities succinctly

As you assign responsibilities to objects, enter them in the left-hand side of the object's class card. It's a good idea to keep responsibility descriptions short and simple. Just jot down a well-chosen phrase that captures the essence of the responsibility. The scribe can record the thinking behind the responsibility in case the phrase turns out to be too cryptic.

Think of objects as living entities

Getting data-oriented modelers to think in terms of proactive objects can be a challenge. A good way to break old modes of thinking is to encourage modelers to anthropomorphize objects—to think of them as living beings who are responsible for carrying out their duties as efficiently as possible. This approach not only leads to more self-managing objects, it also encourages a spirit of fun in the design process. For example, a product would be modeled in a data design as a collection of related information. But a Product *object* can be given the power to compute its own price, forecast its sales, reorder itself, and look out for its interests in a variety of different ways.

Assign responsibilities logically and evenly

When assigning responsibilities to objects, there are two main criteria to bear in mind. First, you should strive to distribute responsibilities logically, in the sense that you shouldn't ask an object to know or do something outside of its normal scope. For example, you could reasonably expect a Product object to project its future sales, but it would not be reasonable to have it project the sales of other products. Second, you should try to assign responsibilities evenly, so that all objects are fully responsible for their own actions rather than having a few "control" objects with many responsibilities and a host of "data" objects with very few responsibilities.

As you attempt to assign responsibilities in a way that meets these criteria, you may find yourself migrating responsibilities from one object to another, discovering new objects, or wondering whether two objects that you thought were different should be merged. This rethinking is a natural part of assigning responsibilities, and constructive redefinition of objects should be taken as a sign of progress.

Be on the look-out for new objects

The Dylan team decides to start by trying to understand how it should model customers. It immediately concludes that the Customer object should be responsible for knowing its name, address, and shipping information, as well as any other data that might be required by operations. It also decides that a Customer should know its current balance and its payment status so that the company can be cautious about extending further credit if a customer is in arrears.

Modeling the Customer class

Having assigned these information-oriented responsibilities, the team is tempted to move on. But the facilitator reminds the group that a Customer object should not just represent the passive characteristics of a real-world customer, but it should be an active software agent that helps the company manage its interactions with that customer. The team is not quite sure what else the Customer object should do, but Jean Sutherland has a pro-

Animating the Customer

The Customer class.

Customer	CLASS
Know name, addresses, etc.	
Know assigned Salesperson	
Know discount schedule	
Know balance & payment status	
Issue statements	
Collect past-due amounts	
Record/report history of sales	
Project sales by products	

posal—make the Customer responsible for keeping track of prior sales and projecting future sales on a product-by-product basis. She likes this idea because it would support much more precise sales forecasting than the spreadsheet models that Dylan is currently using. The group concurs, and the responsibility is added.

Self-billing Customers

Bill Johnson now suggests a responsibility that really surprises the team. He wants Customer objects to issue statements to their real-world counterparts and handle the collections process. Bill wants this feature because the company has a great deal of money tied up in overdue accounts. Dylan's accounting system is of no help here—it can generate invoices and print out aging reports, but it has no means of following up on late payments. Bill reasons that if a Customer object is going to know its payment status, there is no reason not to have the Customer tell the accounting system when to send statements and then follow up as needed with periodic reminders of increasing intensity. According to some quick calculations on Bill's part, this feature alone could pay for the system within six months. End of discussion.

Fractal Customers

One of the object modelers points out that Customer is a good candidate for a fractal object. Dylan deals with a number of national companies that have regional and city offices. By nesting Customers within Customers, as shown in the next figure, Dylan could represent these multisite customers much more efficiently than it currently does using multiple ship-to addresses. Jean Sutherland is quick to point out that this structure would also allow Customers to project their sales at every level, from cities to regions to the company as a whole. The team is convinced, and a fractal collection of component Customers is added to the Customer card.

Fractal Customers.

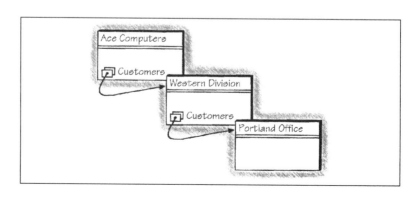

When the team reaches the Product class another interesting discussion takes place. One of the object modelers argues that Products should be responsible for replenishing themselves. This idea makes sense—it just takes the group a while to get used to it. Carol Williams clinches the argument by pointing out that Products can roll up the sales forecasts generated by Customers, allowing each Product to fine tune its orders to minimize inventory while avoiding backorders wherever possible. Here again, the obvious business benefit closes the debate.

Products order themselves

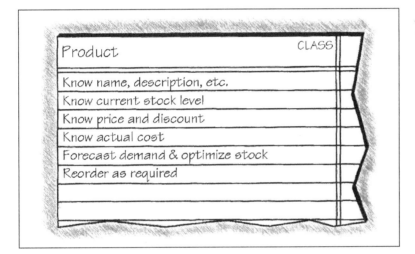

Responsibilities for the Product class.

Defining Relationships

Class cards have areas for entering information about each of the three major types of relationship, as shown in the next illustration. For collaborations, place the names of the collaborators—the objects that are called upon for services—on the same line as the responsibilities they support. For superclasses, simply enter the name of the superclass as soon as it is known. Use the bottom of the card to list the components of composite objects.

Capture the three key relationships

The composition of Dylan's SalesDepartment has already been well defined, but one of the object modelers points out that the SalesDepartment should be able to access all of the company's Customers. The team agrees with this observation and decides to place a collection in the SalesDepartment to contain references to all the Customers. But Jean argues that each salesperson needs

Accessing customers quickly

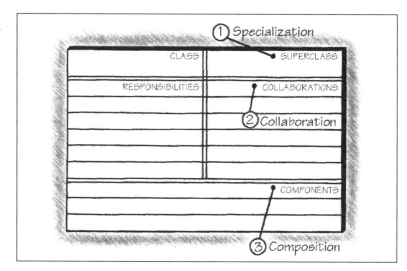

rapid access to his or her own customers, and that the only efficient way to provide this is to place the appropriate subset of
Customers inside each Salesperson object. Marty concurs but
points out a problem with Jean's approach—when a customer
calls in, the system will have to search through every Salesperson object in order to find the right Customer object and
route the call accordingly.

*Defining two
access routes*

After some debate, the team realizes that it is dealing with a
simple performance trade-off. The system will behave correctly
no matter where Customers are placed, but either decision will
lead to slower response under some conditions. The team
doesn't like the idea of giving up performance in either case, so it
elects to use both strategies. A large collection containing all
Dylan Customers is placed in the SalesDepartment, and smaller
collections for the Customers managed by each salesperson are
placed in the corresponding Salesperson object. The resulting
design is shown in the next figure.

*Modeling sales
orders*

In thinking through how Customers will order Products, the
Dylan team soon discovers it has overlooked an important
object—a SalesOrder. The SalesOrder is the place where the
products being sold are listed and a total price computed. In
examining the responsibilities and collaborations of this class, the
team quickly realizes that SalesOrders need to have line items to
handle orders for multiple products. This leads to the creation of

a LineItem class, which must handle information about quantity, product, description, price, and extended price. The SalesOrder consists of (1) header, with customer and shipping information; (2) a collection of line items; and (3) a footer, which totals up the order.

Pricing turns out to be the most complex responsibility of SalesOrders. Each LineItem must request the price of its Product, then multiply by the quantity to get an extended price. But any discounts that apply to the Product, including both specials and volume discounts, must be taken into account. These prices must be rolled up across all LineItems and totaled in the footer of the SalesOrder. If a Customer has any discounts that apply, these must be factored into the total price as well. The pattern of collaborations to compute the total price is shown in the next figure.

*Pricing
SalesOrders*

You should explore special cases of your basic classes just far enough to make sure that the needs of the business will be met by the model. For example, you may start out with a single product object. But suppose you offered both goods and services, which would be sold and billed in very different ways. These two types of product would be sufficiently different that they would require explicit modeling during the initial design session, and they should be broken out as separate classes before doing any more work with the product object.

*Explore special
cases at the
business level*

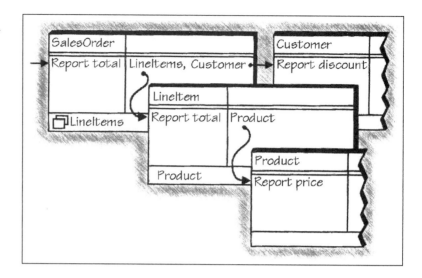

Order Subclasses

Marty Klein points out that much of the logic developed for SalesOrders applies equally to PurchaseOrders, so the group rapidly fills in the composition and collaborations of the PurchaseOrder class. After this process is completed, one of the object modelers points out that the responsibilities that appear in both the SalesOrder and PurchaseOrder classes could be captured in a single class called Order, then inherited by these two special cases. That would reduce the amount of programming required to construct these classes, it would facilitate change, and it would make it easy to add new types of Orders in the future. Jean observes that backorders and special orders are actually variations on the basic sales order, so she suggests that these be modeled as subclasses of SalesOrder. This results in the hierarchy of Order classes shown in the following figure. Rather than deal with creating the new classes right now, the team charges the object modelers with completing this task during the drill-down phase.

Dylan Distributors

As the design takes shape, the team discovers that it has three top-level objects, all of which are Departments of Dylan Distributors. Only now does it really sink in that the group is building a true model of its company. To reflect this insight, the team declares one additional class, DylanDistributors, and uses it as an all-encompassing composite object. This new class provides a context for future development as other teams model other departments and processes. It will normally be a class with

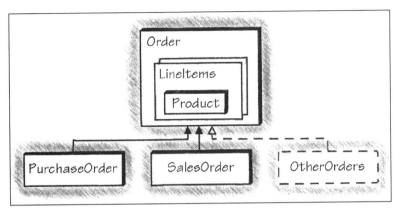

a single instance because there is only one Dylan Distributors in
the real world. However, copies of this single instance may be
generated and executed off line for simulation purposes.

Validating the Model

In responsibility-driven design, a model is tested for correctness
and completeness many times before a line of code is ever written. The basic technique is for a design team to "walk through"
the operation of the model under various conditions, making
sure the model demonstrates the appropriate behavior in all

*Validate a
design using
walk-throughs*

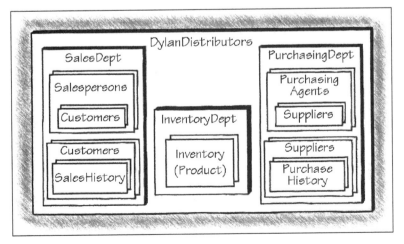

cases. The actual mechanics of these walk-throughs may vary over time, increasing in rigor as the model is refined through testing. The recommended progression is shown in the following diagram and described in subsequent sections. The class cards developed by the Dylan team at this point are shown in the Appendix. You may wish to conduct your own walk-throughs using these cards to better understand the process.

Sequence of walk-through techniques.

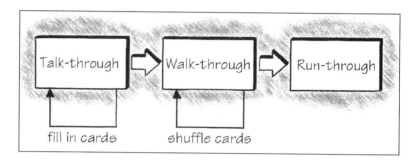

Talk-throughs keep the cards on the table

The first form of a walk-through is more appropriately termed a *talk-through*. In a talk-through, the class cards remain on the table where the entire team can see them, refer to them by gesture, and edit them as required. Talk-throughs are used primarily to test the basic logic of the design and make sure it can handle the critical business scenarios. As each scenario is "executed" by the model, the team examines each collaboration in turn to verify that the required operations are carried out correctly. Depending on the complexity of the design, the team may require from 2 to 10 attempts to get a successful talk-through of any given scenario, revising its design after each attempt.

Talk-throughs identify services

The most challenging part of talk-throughs is deciding how each object will provide services to other objects. The responsibilities listed on the class card cover the entire span of knowledge and activities within the object. As you talk through the collaborations, you should begin to explore which of these responsibilities is reflected in services and how these services might be requested by other objects. This discussion lays the foundation for the formal definition of service interfaces in the detailing activities described in Chapter 6. In the design session, the emphasis should not be on detail but on general flow. The scribe should make extensive notes for each class during this period to make sure the team's conclusions are captured. The notes shown with the classes in the Appendix illustrate the kind of information the scribe should record.

Once the model survives its talk-through tests, the class cards are distributed to individual team members, who will use the cards as informal "scripts" to role-play the behavior of the objects. In this capacity, participants narrate the actions they take as individual objects, and they speak to each other by sending verbal messages to trigger collaborations. These walk-throughs represent a tougher test for the design because the sequence of collaborations is more rigorously enforced. They also offer a healthy change of pace for the modelers because walk-throughs are very interactive and can lead to some humorous situations as the designers try to figure out what their objects are supposed to be doing.

Walk-throughs are based on role playing

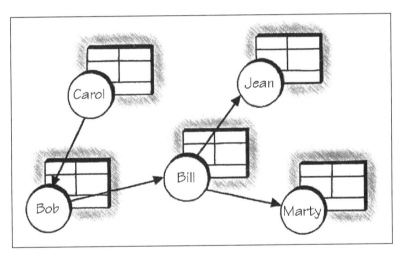

Modelers role-playing objects.

The final step, the run-through, is a faster version of a walk-through in which only object communications are permitted, with no "offline" discussions or on-the-spot debugging of the design. By the time the design is ready for a run-through, it should be fully debugged and require only a final quality check. The run-through is also an opportunity for team members to enjoy the fruits of their labors. After the intense effort required to create a sophisticated business model, it can be quite rewarding to put the model through its paces and actually experience the objects performing their tasks in clockwork fashion.

The run-through is the final quality check

Identify with the objects

Modelers should "assume the identity" of the objects they role-play in these walk-throughs. They should constantly question whether they should be responsible for a particular task, when they should call on other objects for help, and what else they might do to be more responsible contributors to the business process. This identification with objects often leads to animated negotiations over responsibilities as some modelers attempt to garner more power for their objects or dispose of responsibilities they don't want to bother with. If individual personalities start to interfere with the appropriate balancing of responsibilities, shuffle the cards and change who plays which object.

Pass a token to track messages

Certain techniques can make these walk-throughs easier and more productive. It is helpful to write the name of each object on the back of its card in large letters so that the now-human "objects" can easily locate each other. It also helps to have participants get up from the table and stand in a pattern that replicates the original layout of the cards so that the spatial format of collaborations is preserved. Another useful technique is to use a token of some kind, such as a whiteboard marker, to keep track of the "thread" of messages in the interacting model. As each "object" receives a request to carry out some action, the token is passed to that person, who may in turn pass it to some other object as part of its response to the request. The token must always retrace its path as objects eventually respond to the messages sent to them after fulfilling their responsibilities.

Tracing the walk-throughs

As the team conducts each walk-through, the scribe captures the sequence of messages and actions that each object executes. A good notation for this trace is an indented list, where each shift to the right corresponds to a new object receiving a request for services and taking control. As objects return control to the objects that called them, the list shifts back to the left again. Given this convention, you can always tell which object is in control by looking at the name of the object above the list of events. In the following example, a Property object calculates its debt-to-value ratio by sending messages to two loans outstanding against the property.

> *Property,* calculate debtToValue
>   (Property discovers that it has two loans against it)
> *Loan1,* calculate payoff
>   (Loan1 returns the principal amount)

Loan2, calculate payoff
  (Loan2 does the same but adds a prepayment penalty)
  (Property divides its value by the sum of the two amounts)
  (Property returns the ratio in response to the request)

As the preceding example illustrates, it helps to show messages by placing a comma between the receiver of a message and the service being requested. This notation makes the trace easier to read because it corresponds to the way people make requests of each other ("John, please have a seat"). Internal actions of an object that do not involve messages are best shown in parentheses for clarity.

Clarify messages and actions

Walk-throughs are based on actual run-time objects, not classes. This distinction is important because classes are simply definitions for objects, and there may be multiple instances of a class active in the model at any given time. In this case, have a different person role-play each instance of the class. This avoids the confusion of having one person playing the roles of multiple objects, and it can help clarify the actual creation of individual run-time objects.

Role-play objects, not classes

The Dylan team runs into exactly this problem when it attempts to role-play the actions of a SalesOrder. Each SalesOrder contains multiple LineItems, each of which refers to a different product. Initially, a single person is assigned to play the role of LineItem, but that becomes much too confusing. To clear up the confusion, the team assigns three people to be LineItem objects, each representing a different product. The team then works through all the services of a SalesOrder using these three LineItems to ensure that they work correctly. Once this test is complete, SalesOrders are assumed to work properly in subsequent walk-throughs and are no longer exercised in detail.

Testing a SalesOrder

The following trace shows the sequence of messages and actions recorded as the team tests filling out a sales order. The SalesOrder itself is assumed to be driven by a human salesperson, who clicks buttons on a screen to request services of the SalesOrder. In constructing a new SalesOrder, only three services are involved: filling in the header, adding as many line items as are required and requesting the SalesOrder to complete the footer with its discounts, taxes, and totals. These services can be called in any order by the salesperson by clicking the appropriate

Tracing the SalesOrder scenario

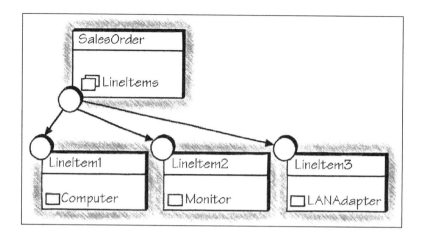

buttons. The same logic applies to PurchaseOrders, so testing one tests them both.

> *SalesOrder,* fill in header
> *Customer,* supply shipping address
> (SalesOrder enters this information in header area)
> *SalesOrder,* add a line item
> (SalesOrder creates a new *LineItem* and adds it to *LineItems*)
> *LineItem,* accept *Product* (as selected by the user)
> *LineItem,* accept quantity (as entered by the user)
> *Product,* report quantity discounted price
> *SalesOrder,* fill in footer
> *Customer,* report your discount
> **LineItems,** total extended prices
> (SalesOrder applies discount and adds shipping)

Tackling a top-level scenario

Now that SalesOrders and PurchaseOrders are known to work, the team can test its top-level scenarios. Execution of the first scenario, placing an order, is triggered by an incoming call to the sales department. As the scenario begins, an operator in the sales department has taken a call, identified the customer, and selected that customer's name from a list on the screen. This action sends the initial message to the SalesDepartment object:

> *SalesDepartment,* route an incoming call
> *Customer,* report your assigned *Salesperson*
> *Salesperson,* accept this sales call
> (Salesperson brings up the sales screen)

Customer, report basic info and sales history
    (Salesperson displays this information)
    (Salesperson creates a new *SalesOrder*)
SalesOrder, fill in header
SalesOrder, fill in line item 1
SalesOrder, fill in line item 2
SalesOrder, fill in line item 3
SalesOrder, fill in the footer
InventoryDepartment, verify inventory
    (User gives verbal quote to customer & gets agreement)
SalesOrder, print the order form
InventoryDepartment, ship the products
    (Salesperson returns control to the SalesDepartment)

Final run-throughs

By Friday morning, the Dylan team is able to run through its basic scenarios quickly and smoothly. In addition, it has identified half a dozen pockets of local collaborations that require testing, such as the execution of SalesOrder services, and it has completed run-throughs of these as well. The team concludes that it has a solid working model and devotes the afternoon to discussing issues that are bound to arise during the detailing of the model. These informal discussions mark the transition to the third and final stage of developing the business design.

6

Detailing a Business Design

The final step in the design process is driving the model down to a lower level of detail and preparing it for implementation. This activity is done after the completion of the design week and involves the people from the business side only if questions of business consequence arise. The critical activity is translating each responsibility into methods that can fulfill the responsibility. The collaborations that support each responsibility are expressed as messages to other objects within these methods. Finally, implementation decisions are made based on the requirements of the detailed design, including both technology choices and decisions regarding how best to leverage legacy systems. Because the detailing process is a relatively technical activity, business readers may elect to skip this chapter and move directly to Part 3.

Defining Service Interfaces

The detailing process begins with the definition of service interfaces for each class. The service interface consists of all the methods that can be called by other classes. For each method that appears in the service interface, you must specify the name of the method, any parameters it requires for execution, and the type of value returned by the method. Once defined, these service interfaces are made available to other objects. This interface

Define service interfaces first

87

is all that any object can ever know about another object within the model.

Services of the Customer class

The Dylan modelers begin by translating the responsibilities of their Customer class into services. An issue immediately arises concerning the "Know balance and payment status" responsibility. The modelers are fairly confident that the Customer object will contain a variable for the current balance and a variable for the payment status, so defining a few "get" and "set" methods ought to suffice. But that interpretation of the responsibility would violate the encapsulation of the Customer object and rob it of important responsibilities. After some discussion, the modelers decide that the Customer object should simply be able to process payments. Its only services for balance and status is to report them. How it manages this information is its own business.

Summarizing the service interface

The modelers elect to show parameters in parentheses and to use braces to show alternative responses that can be drawn from a list of alternatives. For example, the service *reportStatus* returns one of three states: *current, late,* or *delinquent.* The group adopts the notation {*outcome*} to indicate that the requested service was either carried out successfully or that a specified problem was encountered. The following figure illustrates how a few of the responsibilities are expressed in this notation.

Selected services for the Customer class.

```
Know balance and payment status
     reportStatus → {current, late, delinquent}
     reportBalance → dollarAmount
     acceptPayment(amount,date) → {outcome}
Record sales history
     recordSale(SalesOrder) → {outcome}
     reportSalesFor(period) → collection of SalesOrders
Project sales trends by product
     projectSalesFor(period) → dollarAmount
     projectSalesOf(product,period) → quantity

                    ⋮
```

Once they complete the first few classes, the object modelers find that they can define the service interfaces much more rapidly. They quickly move through the other classes, then test their new interfaces by performing another run-through. In this run-through, the modelers confine all their interactions to "object-speak," explicitly invoking named services with sample parameter values and accepting a return value in response. The team makes numerous adjustments to its interfaces as it discovers missing services, changes parameters, or eliminates services that violate encapsulation.

Testing service interfaces

Exploring Special Cases

The process of defining service interfaces is bound to uncover examples of specialization that were not apparent during the modeling session. How this specialization is handled during the detailing phase depends on how the special cases differ from each other. As shown in the following figure, specialization can be expressed at three different levels: the service interface, the implementation of service methods, and the values of data.

Define subclasses as required

Three levels of specialization.

Level of Specialization	Method of Handling
Different service interfaces	Model subclasses in design session
Different implementations for same services	Drill down subclasses in detailing phase
Different data values only	Model using instances, not classes

One of the objectives of the detailing process should be to implement special cases at the lowest possible level in the preceding figure. If all the variations among product objects can be dealt

Implement special cases as simply as possible

with by placing different values in their variables, then a single Product class is all that is required. If the variations among products require different ways of carrying out services, then different subclasses of Product will be required at the implementation level but need not be visible at the level of the business model. If the variations among products are so great that they require different service interfaces, then they must appear in the business model in order to make it understandable.

Serialized and non-serialized products

In detailing the Dylan design, the object modelers discover that the business team lumped two different kinds of objects together in the Product class—serialized and non-serialized products. The difference is not very important at the business level and should be as transparent as possible. At the implementation level, however, the difference is significant and must be dealt with. Serialized products, such as computers and monitors, must be tracked for service and warranty purposes. By contrast, electronic supplies, such as transistors, are purchased in batches and are treated as equivalent.

Solving the problem through subclassing

The object modelers deal with this problem by declaring two subclasses of Product, SerializedProduct and NonSerialized-Product. The two subclasses have the same service interface and are interchangeable at the level of the business model. But the way they carry out their services differs significantly. The NonSerializedProduct simply keeps a running total of the stock on hand and replenishes this stock as required. By contrast, the SerializedProduct class creates an instance of an IndividualProduct for every product that moves through Dylan Distributors. Each IndividualProduct knows its own serial number, purchase date, specifications, disposition, and service history.

Polymorphism at work

In short, the object modelers handled this specialization problem at the intermediate level, providing two different implementations of the same service interface. Because the two subclasses of Product are hidden behind a common interface, they can be used interchangeably in the business model. This is another example of how polymorphism can simplify a business design. Any combination of products can be purchased, sold, and serviced without worrying about whether or not they are serialized. The class definitions for each product will automatically take care of the special handling required by serialized products. Moreover, the fact that the distinction between the two is transparent means

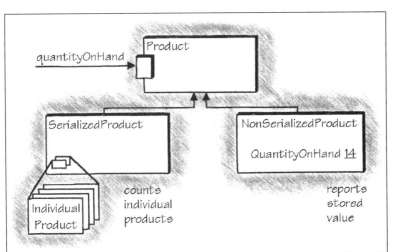

that Dylan can easily move products to and from serialized control without disturbing the operation of the business model.

A business design can be simplified by working up the inheritance hierarchy as well as down it. Whenever you have two or more classes that appear to have services in common, you should examine those classes to see whether they can be expressed as subclasses of a more general purpose superclass. If they can, then move all the common functionality up to this new class. This eliminates redundancy in the design, promotes internal reuse, and simplifies changes in future versions of the model.

Invent super-classes to simplify the design

Classes that exist only to capture generic characteristics are often referred to as *abstract classes*. Abstract classes are actually a common, everyday tool for expressing general concepts in a convenient form. For example, we use the term "animal" to refer to a great variety of living things, but there are no actual instances of animals in the real world. There are only instances of the subclasses of animal—lions, tigers, penguins, and people. Similarly, abstract classes in object technology exist only to reflect commonalities and they, too, have no instances. However, there is no real difference in the way abstract classes are defined, and it is possible to make an abstract class concrete at any time simply by using it to define instances.

Abstract classes have no instances

91

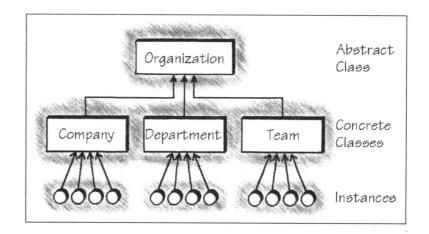

Abstract Class

Concrete Classes

Instances

Dylan's abstract classes

The Dylan design team already discovered one abstract class—the Order class. This class exists only to capture the commonalities among SalesOrders and PurchaseOrders, including the way they handle their component LineItems. In detailing the design, the object modelers discover three additional abstract classes that simplify the model: Company, Department, and Employee. For each of these abstract classes, the modelers look for characteristics that are common to all the subclasses and move them up into the abstract class.

Dylan's other abstract classes.

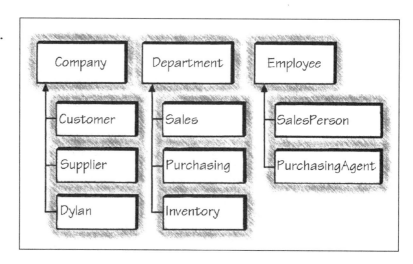

Specialization through subclassing is a powerful tool on both the conceptual and implementation levels. This power can work for or against you, depending on how carefully you wield it. Improperly used, subclassing can cause more problems than it solves. The most common error is to use subclassing merely to reuse code. Internal code reuse is an excellent reason for using subclassing, but if it's the *only* reason, you will very likely create inscrutable class hierarchies that produce undesirable side effects whenever high-level classes are changed. To avoid this pitfall, use subclassing only if the following conditions are met:

Use subclassing carefully

1. The proposed subclass is truly a special case of its super-class as generally understood at the business level.

2. You want the subclass to inherit all possible changes in its superclass, including changes in features that don't even exist yet.

3. You have examined the alternatives to subclassing and none of them does the job as well as subclassing.

Alternatives to Subclassing

One alternative to subclassing is *switching*. When the difference between two potential subclasses is quite minor, keying off a single piece of information, it is often simpler to place a flag or "switch" variable that triggers the appropriate response. For example, if you want the option of declaring reports to be confidential, you could set a confidentiality variable to TRUE or FALSE and have the object behave accordingly.

Use switching for simple variations

Switching is particularly appropriate when the difference being captured is really one of *state* rather than *type*. The distinction between the two can be subtle, but the basic question to be asked is whether a single type of object is simply moving from one state to another. There may be many types of reports in a business system, including financial reports, project plans, progress reports, sales summaries, and product comparisons. Some of these reports would initially be confidential and others would not, but all would have the possibility of moving to and from confidential status over time. Given these considerations, confidentiality is best regarded as a state of a report rather than a type of report.

Switching is good for state changes

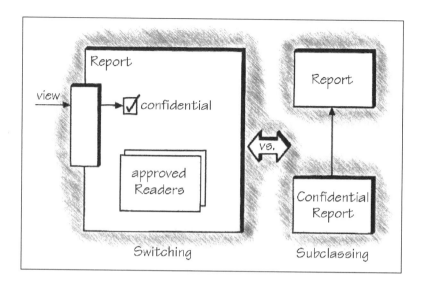

Switching   Subclassing

Delegation is another alternative

Another alternative to subclassing is delegation. Instead of gaining reuse through inheritance from a superclass, delegation achieves reuse by including a component object that carries out the required services. Delegation is a powerful mechanism, and it represents the only viable alternative when a composite object is required to carry out tasks that properly belong to its components.

Delegating the computation of discounts

In the Dylan design, a Customer is responsible for calculating its own corporate discount. Dylan already has several different discounting programs available to its customers, and it wants to expand its range of options dynamically in order to match new programs introduced by its competitors. The object modelers don't want to embed the methods for handling all these different programs within the Customer object, nor do they want to create subclasses of the Customer object based on discounts. Their solution is to create a hierarchy of Discounter classes and place an instance of the appropriate type in each Customer. The task of computing a discount is then delegated to the Discounter object currently assigned to that Customer. If necessary, the Discounter can interview the Customer object to get additional information before returning the amount of the discount.

Object morphing offers new possibilities

Another technique to be considered is *object morphing,* in which a single class is able to transform itself from one form to another based on the values of its variables. In essence, object morphing

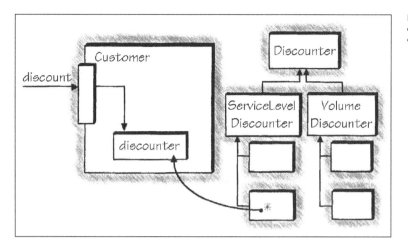

is an extension of switching in which one or more variables may take on a full range of values, transforming the characteristics of the object in the process. The power of object morphing is that it allows a single class to do the work of many. It also allows any given object to alter its behavior dynamically to accommodate changing requirements.

The Dylan team is faced with a difficult problem that was completely glossed over in the business design session. Products come packaged in a wide range of containers, including boxes, cartons, and pallets. Depending on the product, zero, one, two, or all three of these levels of packaging may be applicable. The problem is how to handle packaging information within the Product class without having to create a huge variety of subclasses to handle all the special cases. The solution is to define a Package object that contains a set number of products. By nesting Packages in a fractal manner and giving them different names, it is possible to handle all possible combinations of packaging types and quantities.

Morphing packages

Using this scheme, a single Product object can morph all the way from unit shipments to multiple levels of packaging. Reducing the package size to one at any level automatically drops that level out, allowing any combination of packaging to be accepted with any shipment. Packages of mixed quantity can also be handled in this system because each package knows its own quantity. Finally, the process of breaking packages can be fully encapsu-

Hiding package operations

95

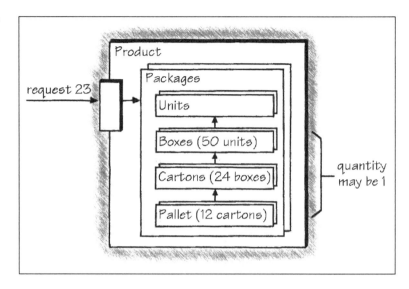

lated within the Product object. When asked for a given number of units, a Product will automatically examine its available packages, shipping the largest packages possible to make up the order, and breaking packages as necessary to fill out odd lots.

Interacting with Legacy Systems

Review the legacy systems again

Once the design of the model is complete and is able to meet its business goals, it's time to revisit the legacy systems to determine what can be carried forward. The added information for this second evaluation is the way functionality is packaged in the model. If the functions of a legacy system end up being packaged in one component of the model or if they lie outside the model altogether, then keeping the legacy system intact becomes a more attractive option. If the functions of the legacy system are spread throughout the model or packaged in ways that fundamentally contradict the construction of the model, then the legacy systems will be difficult to preserve.

Preserve as much as you can

The goal in this final review is to preserve as much functionality as you can without compromising the integrity of the new business model. This is the way to achieve the biggest return on the smallest investment in development dollars. An ideal scenario would be to construct a set of object-oriented business models that significantly increase the flexibility you have in the way you do business yet rely on legacy systems for 80 to 90 percent of the actual computing work. How close you can come to this ideal depends on many factors, including the accessibility and flexibility of your legacy systems.

In reviewing their earlier conclusions, the Dylan modelers discover no difficulties in pursuing the original plan for how they will use their legacy systems. The two sales tools can be dropped as planned—the functionality of the Sales Assistant will be provided by the new, integrated model, and the job of sales forecasting will be carried out by the Customer objects. The Product Control System can also be dropped because all Product objects know their own levels, locations, and other critical information. As planned, the accounting and warehouse systems will remain intact, with no modifications.

Dylan's legacy systems

Implementing these decisions requires establishing the interfaces shown in the following diagram. The SalesDepartment and PurchasingDepartment require write access to the Sales and Purchasing modules, respectively, in order to get these activities into the accounting system. Similarly, the InventoryDepartment must be able to write to the inventory module of the accounting system to keep it up to date. The Product Control System being replaced currently writes to the accounting system using keyboard emulation, and the modelers use this same technique with the new object design. Finally, the output of the Warehouse System can simply be diverted from the old Product Control System to the InventoryDepartment of the object model.

Accessing the systems

It is important to hide the fact that you are accessing legacy systems. The best technique for doing this is to limit the number of objects that access existing systems and to hide that access within these objects. This approach will make it as easy as possible to move legacy functions up into these objects at a later date without disturbing the model as a whole.

Hide all access to legacy systems

The Dylan modelers encapsulate all access to their legacy systems in three objects: SalesOrder, PurchaseOrder, and Product. The SalesOrder and PurchaseOrder objects are responsible for passing information into the sales and purchasing modules of the accounting system, respectively. The Product object reads infor-

Hiding legacy access

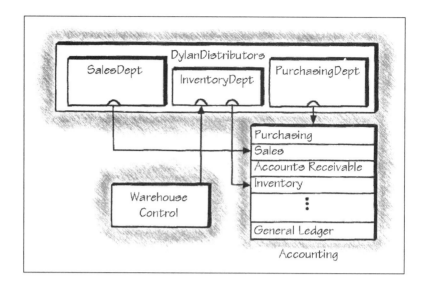

mation about the location and quantity of products from the
Warehouse System and provides updates to the accounting system. When Dylan gets around to replacing its Warehouse
Control System, it will simply add a Warehouse object into its
model of the company. So long as access from existing objects to
this new warehouse model is through Product objects, the rest
of the business model will be unaffected by the transition.

*Move off legacy
systems
gradually*

The major benefit of hiding all access to legacy systems is that it
allows a company to make a graceful transition to object technology. If your legacy systems permit this strategy, you can start out
by building a very thin shell of object-oriented business models
that use the legacy code to do most of the work. Gradually, on an
opportunistic basis, you can migrate functionality out of the
legacy systems and into the object models. Over time, the object
shell will grow thicker and the legacy core will shrink. You can
make the changeover as quickly or as slowly as your needs and
resources dictate without ever disrupting the operation of your
object-oriented business models.

Making Implementation Decisions

*Choose a lan-
guage to fit the
model*

Given that convergent engineering is language-independent, a
modeling team doesn't need to know the language in which a
model or system will be implemented. This not only produces

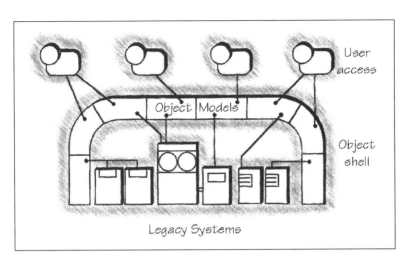

more generic, reusable designs, it allows the team to postpone implementation decisions until after the design is complete. That way the requirements of the model can help determine the choice of languages. An additional benefit of language-independent design is that it is possible to build models that remain stable as the feature sets of the available languages continue to evolve.

Choosing a language

Dylan Distributors wants to avoid any risk of building its system on a language that may not survive, so it restricts its selection to languages that have large installed bases and three or more independent vendors. Only two languages pass these tests: C++ and SmallTalk. After comparing the strengths and weaknesses of the two languages, the company decides to build its high-level business model in SmallTalk. Its choice is dictated by the dynamic flexibility of the language and the speed with which systems can be developed. It realizes that it may be making some performance trade-offs, but it regards the cost of processing power as small compared to the business benefits it expects to realize.

99

Mixing languages

The company also decides to revisit the language decision when it replaces the Warehouse Control System. This system deals with real-time machine control, which argues against the use of a language that can perform time-consuming "garbage collection" (memory recovery) at unpredictable times. Given that the warehouse system will run on a separate machine from the core business system, the use of a different language, although inconvenient, would be manageable.

Choose databases based on requirements	The choice of a storage medium for objects should also be based on the requirements of the design. In general, there are two main candidates: object databases and relational databases. It is possible to use flat file systems, and it is also possible to store objects in network or hierarchical databases. But flat files are of little use in multiuser business systems, and the older network and hierarchical database management systems are quite rigid and would make it very difficult to change the structure of a class once it had been defined. In practice, object and relational database management systems (DBMSs) are the only viable options.
Relational systems are a safer choice	The more conservative option is the relational DBMS. Relational technology has been commercially available for over 15 years and is now reasonably mature and robust. Relational DBMSs have also been demonstrated to scale comfortably up to hundreds of users and tens of gigabytes. By contrast, object DBMSs are still relatively new, they are still maturing as commercial products, and some vendors are still struggling with scalability issues.
Object systems are a better fit	The flip side of the argument is that object DBMSs provide a much more natural form of storage for object technology. In order to use a relational database to store objects, objects must be "decomposed" into relational form and recomposed upon retrieval. For base-level (non-composite) objects, this translation process can be quite fast. For deeply nested composite objects, it can be painfully slow, dragging access speeds down by one to two orders of magnitude.
Database types can be mixed	As with languages, there is no requirement to adopt a single type of database technology for all the objects in a system. If objects are made responsible for their own persistence, updating their stored representations whenever their state changes, then each object is free to use the most appropriate form of storage technology. However, mixing database types may require some functions normally handled by the DBMS be taken care of within the object model. This approach works best when there is little or no interaction between the objects that are stored in the two different kinds of systems.
Choosing a DBMS technology	Dylan Distributors has the advantage that it is a medium-sized company and deals with a relatively limited set of customers. Given these characteristics, scalability is not as important as per-

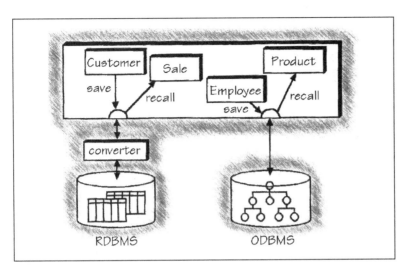

formance, and the company opts to go with an object DBMS. However, it does reserve the option of moving objects representing Sales and Purchases to a relational database during the deployment phase if scaling considerations dictate this move. All the other objects in its model are characterized by relatively low volume and high complexity, so the object DBMS offers a much better fit in these cases.

Reviewing the Model

At this point, Dylan Distributors has a model of their core business operations that is ready for construction and deployment. The model achieves its basic goals in that it provides a framework for simplifying and optimizing the basic sales and purchasing functions of the company. Moreover, the design takes maximum advantage of Dylan's existing systems while providing a smooth migration path toward a fully integrated business system in future years.

Assessing the model

101

Perhaps most importantly, the model provides a vehicle for moving Dylan Distributors away from conventional application development into the new era of convergent engineering. The model they have designed will allow Dylan to become an evolutionary business that can change dynamically in response to

The move to convergent engineering

changing needs. This evolutionary capability will give Dylan a profound competitive advantage as the company quickly adapts to changing business conditions that leave other companies wondering what happened to their market share.

Extending the model

The Dylan object modelers could stop the design process here and begin coding their system. However, the techniques they have used to date represent only the most fundamental aspects of convergent engineering. Like the companies it supports, convergent engineering is itself constantly evolving and extending its capabilities. The third section of this book describes some extensions of convergent engineering that increase its power to support enterprise development. Now that the Dylan design team has mastered the fundamentals of convergent engineering, they elect to reconvene and examine some of the extensions to this methodology to discover whether there are further optimizations they can make before implementing their model.

PART THREE

Extension

7

A Framework for Business Objects

Although the fundamentals of convergent engineering bring business and software engineering much closer than they have been historically, there can still be a significant gap between business design and object modeling. For example, business engineering typically requires the explicit representation of high-level organizational processes, whereas these processes are represented implicitly in object models as sequences of messages among business entities. Translating between the two kinds of representation is not difficult, but any translation—however small—represents a violation of convergent engineering. This chapter offers some extensions to the methodology that are designed to close the remaining gap and merge business and software engineering into a fully integrated discipline.

The Evolution of Business Engineering

Business engineering has taken many different forms over the years, beginning with Frederick Taylor's scientific management in the early part of this century. At the risk of some simplification, the evolution of thinking about business optimization since that time may be viewed in terms of three generations, as shown in the following figure.

Business engineering has been evolving

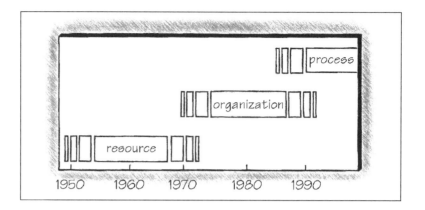

The first generation focused on resources

In the 1950s and 1960s, the emphasis was on *resources.* The implicit assumption was that organizational structure and processes were relatively stable, and the primary goal was to optimize the use of resources consumed by those processes. In the manufacturing arena, this effort produced *material requirements planning (MRP)* systems that addressed the scheduling of raw materials and component parts used in the production of finished goods. The second generation of MRP, *manufacturing resource planning (MRP II),* generalized these systems to include such "fixed" resources as plants, machinery, and workers. Although somewhat dated by modern standards, MRP II remains the foundation technology for many manufacturers. Its concepts have been widely adopted in the service industry as well.

The second generation focused on organization

In the 1970s and 1980s, the emphasis shifted to *organization.* The primary goal has been to move companies from rigid hierarchical structures to flat, dynamic structures that can rapidly regroup in response to changing requirements. In addition to eliminating as many levels of middle management as possible, companies have also eliminated countless staff positions and turned to outsourcing for many activities. The culmination of this trend appears to be the transformation of traditional departments into "centers of excellence" from which ad hoc teams are drawn to carry out the work of the company. Reorganization is still viewed by many companies as the key to increased profitability, and massive "downsizing" efforts continue at many of the nation's leading corporations.

In the 1990s, the emphasis has shifted to *processes*. This latest thrust, known as *business process reengineering (BPR)*, attempts to reduce costs and improve quality by streamlining the critical processes of a company. It has rapidly become the dominant approach to business engineering and is in widespread use at this time. Some of the basic techniques of BPR are as follows:

The third generation concentrates on process

- ❏ *Simplifying operations* by eliminating non-essential approvals, reports, and other organizational activities

- ❏ *Reducing cycle times* for all corporate processes, increasing responsiveness while also reducing costs

- ❏ *Increasing value added* in each operation, incrementally enhancing the quality of a delivered product or service

- ❏ *Cutting costs* in corporate operations in ways that don't compromise quality or time to market

- ❏ *Improving reliability* of corporate processes, increasing the consistency and quality of products and services

- ❏ *Tightening vendor relationships* to improve processes that rely on outside resources

- ❏ *Focusing on core competencies* and outsourcing processes in which the company is not "best of breed"

The occurrence of such major shifts in the focus of business engineering indicates that, like many difficult human endeavors, business engineering is subject to fads. The danger of fads is that each successive view emphasizes a different aspect of a whole that can only be understood as an integrated entity. Each approach to business optimization has contributed something of lasting value, and emphasizing one at the expense of the others entails risks that may not be obvious in advance of the effort. Consider the three generations of business engineering in this light:

Each generation represents a different perspective

1. Focusing on *resources* while assuming that organization and processes are fixed has left many companies with rigid, inflexible structures; for example, MRP II has a failure rate in excess of 80 percent, and it usually works well only under very stable business conditions. Few companies enjoy the luxury of a stable competitive environment today.

2. Focusing on *organization* can cripple a company if its processes are not captured and recast as part of its restructuring effort. Many corporations have laid off thousands of middle-level managers, only to discover that they had eliminated the core knowledge of how essential processes were carried out. It is not uncommon to find these same managers acting as consultants to their former employers, often at several times their prior salary.

3. Focusing on *processes* without engineering a supporting organizational structure can lead to highly efficient processes that are defined in a corporate vacuum. Failure rates in excess of 70 percent are frequently quoted for BPR efforts. A significant factor in these failures is the lack of organizational support in terms of ownership, responsibility, and the allocation of resources. In addition, the very existence of organizations requires supporting processes, such as budgeting and personnel management, that are often overlooked in the application of BPR.

An integrated approach is essential

The way to minimize these risks, although challenging in practice, is straightforward in principle—engineer the business in a way that gives equal weight to resources, organization, and process. In keeping with the core principle of convergent engineering, all three aspects of an organization must be represented explicitly and directly in a unified model of the company and its information systems. The remainder of this chapter provides a framework for business modeling that supports this goal.

The Business Element Framework

The framework is based on a hierarchy

The business modeling framework is based on a hierarchy of business objects that establishes common responsibilities for the major entities that comprise an organization. The top node in the hierarchy is the BusinessElement, which defines the responsibilities generic to all the objects in the framework. The three major subclasses of BusinessElement are Organization, Process, and Resource. These basic types of elements are represented using distinctive shapes to make them immediately recognizable in diagrams. The following figure illustrates these basic forms

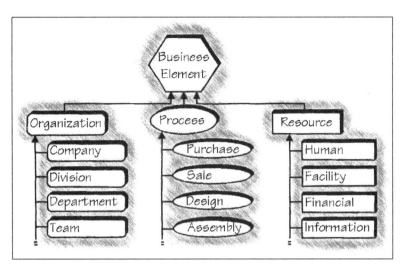

and suggests some possible subclasses for organizations, processes, and resources.

The major categories define each other

The three major subclasses of BusinessElement are heavily dependent on one another. To understand one requires an understanding of the others. The following summary, in conjunction with the next figure, introduces the three categories. Later sections of this chapter deal with each category in turn.

- ❏ *Organizations* are groupings of people and other resources that are tasked with carrying out processes to accomplish goals. Organizations can range from teams to departments to worldwide corporations.

- ❏ *Processes* are sequences of goal-directed activities that consume and generate resources. Examples of organizational processes include buying, selling, negotiating, borrowing, manufacturing, hiring, firing, and subcontracting.

- ❏ *Resources* are assets of the organization that enable processes or are generated by processes. Resources maintain appropriate levels to meet expected demand by interacting with supplier and consumer organizations. Examples of resources include people, equipment, supplies, cash, information, agreements, and capabilities.

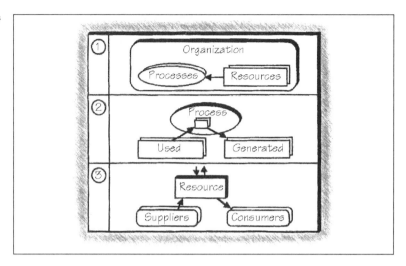

Capabilities of Business Elements

The Business-Element class forms the core

The BusinessElement class defines the capabilities that are common to all the objects in the framework, which are collectively known as business elements. There are four basic capabilities, each of which is explained in the following paragraphs:

1. Supporting simultaneous business activities

2. Scheduling and recording its activities

3. Interacting intelligently with users of a system

4. Managing component objects of the same class

Objects usually operate sequentially

One of the most glaring discrepancies between object-oriented designs and the organizations they represent is that object designs typically assume that only one thing is happening at a time. Only a single object is active at any given moment, and each object waits for a response to a message before commencing any other activity. This assumption is consistent with most contemporary implementations of object technology, but it is a highly unrealistic view of how activities take place in a real-world business. Depending on the size and complexity of a business, many thousands of activities may take place simultaneously. And few real-world objects such as departments and employees cease all activity every time they issue a request for assistance!

If convergent engineering is to produce a model that truly represents the business as well as its software, the model must assume that (1) any number of business elements are capable of simultaneous execution and (2) objects are capable of continuing on with other tasks while waiting for responses to messages they have sent. It does not require that objects actually execute simultaneously at the machine level. That is the ultimate goal, but technology support for this capability is just beginning to become commercially available. The requirement at this point is simply that business designs assume the *possibility* of simultaneous activities so that current implementation constraints are not reflected in the model of the business.

Business elements assume simultaneity

In order to handle potentially simultaneous activities, all business elements are able to schedule future actions and to execute those actions in a timely manner. Business elements are also responsible for maintaining records of their past actions, and they have services for reporting information about their actions over time. These capabilities represent a natural extension of responsibility-driven design, in that objects become responsible for their past and future actions as well as their actions in the moment. Techniques for implementing these capabilities are provided in the final section of this chapter.

Business elements are self-scheduling

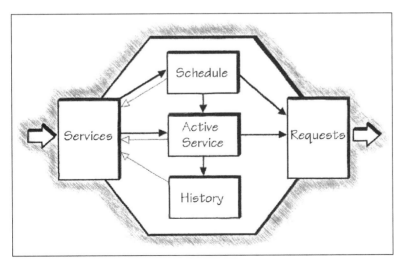

Capabilities of a business element.

111

Business elements are highly autonomous

The ability of business elements to schedule their own activities and monitor their performance allows them to be highly autonomous. With autonomous objects, many routine activities that are normally carried out by people can be delegated to objects. Of course, objects can't think and make decisions—people are still needed to run the company. What self-scheduling elements *can* do is minimize the amount of drudgery that people have to put up with, freeing them to use their time for more intelligent activities such as planning and leading.

Elements ask for help when they need it

When a business element requires a decision from a user of the system, it communicates that need by talking to a Person object that serves as an electronic agent for that user. The Person object queues up requests for intervention and posts them to a screen whenever a user asks to see them. As the user selects each request for viewing, the request is displayed along with the necessary context for making a decision. The user can either supply the decision or take a more active role by reviewing object records, examining the actions of other objects, or intervening in other ways.

Business-Element requesting assistance.

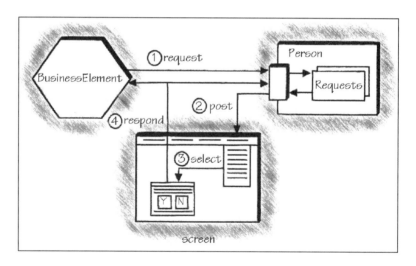

Business elements are inherently fractal

Finally, every business element has the ability to contain and manage other objects of the same type and to cascade services down these components as described in Chapter 3. Each major subclass of BusinessElement has the ability to contain other objects of its own kind. Organization objects can contain other

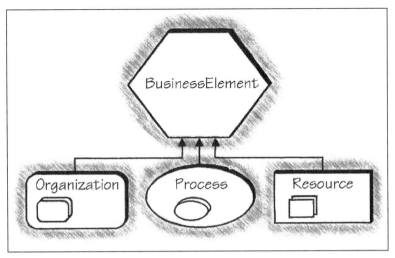

organization objects, processes can contain other processes, and resources can contain other resources.

Capabilities of Organizations

One reason BPR tends to downplay structure is that structure has played too important a role in organizational thinking in years past. Business structures have become too rigid, with lines drawn so sharply that processes often have trouble crossing boundaries. The way to avoid this problem is to allow the binding between organization objects and the other two kinds of objects, processes, and resources to be completely fluid. This leaves a company free to transfer ownership, eliminate barriers, and restructure itself as needed without unduly disrupting operations or resource utilization. At the same time, it maintains a vital infrastructure for handling reporting, budgeting, and the many other management functions that are required for smooth operation.

Organizations are highly dynamic

Because business elements are fractal, organization objects can be nested to any degree. This allows a company to be defined as any desired hierarchy of structures. The following figure shows a classic organizational model for a manufacturing company. Note that the classes Company, Division, BusinessUnit, and

Organizations may be hierarchical

113

Department are all subclasses of Organization, so the structure shown is truly a nesting of organization objects. Forecasting, budgeting, reporting, and other administrative functions common to all organizations are automatically cascaded up and down the hierarchy through fractal composition.

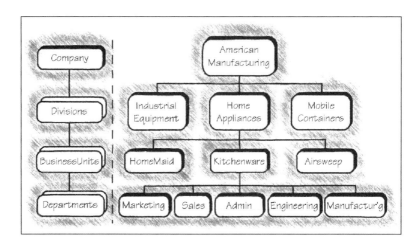

Other organizational models may be used

Although fractal organization objects offer a natural representation of hierarchical management structures, other organizational models are equally well supported. The opposite extreme from the classic hierarchy is the "flat" organization in which departments serve as centers of excellence for staffing dynamically formed teams that carry out the actual work of the company. The next figure shows the same manufacturing company reorganized into action teams that envision new opportunities and carry products all the way from market testing to manufacturing.

Organizations use resources to run processes

The primary responsibility of an organization object is to manage resources in order to carry out its processes in a way that meets its objectives. In general, this will mean conducting those processes as quickly and inexpensively as possible while maintaining quality, but the formula isn't always that simple. For example, maximum speed may not be desirable if there is no advantage in completing processes ahead of schedule.

Organizations manage their own schedules

Organizations fulfill their responsibilities by providing services at the request of other objects. In some cases, these services will be expressed as public methods of the organization. In most cases,

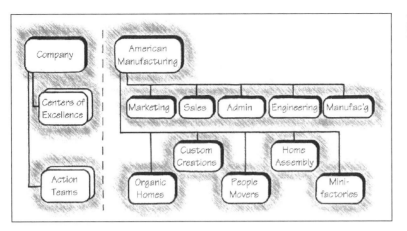

Organizations based on action teams.

however, they will be represented as process objects in order to take advantage of the explicit work-flow capabilities of processes. For a process, the organization first checks to see if it can schedule the required resources to execute the process and its component processes within the requested time frame. If so, the process schedules itself and commits the required resources for the dates on which they will be required. When the process becomes active, it carries out its activities and consumes its resources. Upon completion, it records itself as a completed process to provide an audit trail for the actions of the organization.

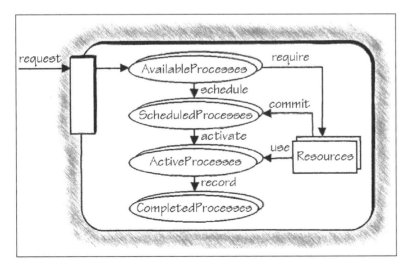

An organization managing its processes.

The responsibilities of organization objects generally support the primary charter to carry out processes as effectively as possible. The organization class should define a common set of services and requests for interacting with other objects. Subclasses of the organization class can override the actual mechanisms for fulfilling these responsibilities. Some recommended responsibilities for an organization are shown in the accompanying figure.

Responsibilities of an organization.

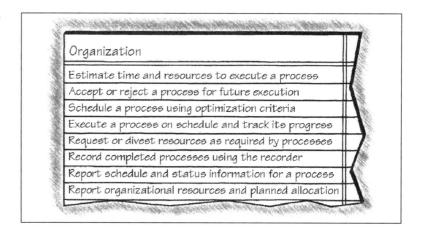

Organization
Estimate time and resources to execute a process
Accept or reject a process for future execution
Schedule a process using optimization criteria
Execute a process on schedule and track its progress
Request or divest resources as required by processes
Record completed processes using the recorder
Report schedule and status information for a process
Report organizational resources and planned allocation

Capabilities of Processes

Business processes must be visible

In most object-oriented design methodologies, processes are not modeled as distinct objects but as sequences of messages moving though a system. An object is requested to perform a service, which triggers one or more requests to other objects, and so on until the goal of the process has been reached. Using this approach to model complex processes that touch many objects can render these processes just as obscure as embedding them in conventional applications. A key aspect of business engineering is defining processes clearly and maintaining their visibility regardless of how they are implemented. Process objects serve this purpose very effectively, and are essential to closing the gap between business engineering and object modeling.

Processes utilize and generate resources

Processes make use of some resources in order to generate other resources. At the most elementary level, the manufacturing process uses cash, labor, supplies, and machine time to create products. Similarly, a marketing program uses market information and other resources to generate prospects for these products. The sales process, in turn, uses prospects and products to generate customers and cash. With good management and a bit of luck, more cash is generated by sales than was consumed by the various processes.

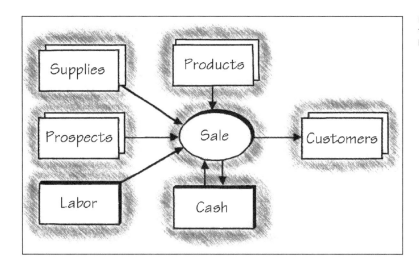

Resources of the sales process.

Like all BusinessElements, process objects are fractal in nature. This means that they can contain other process objects that, in turn, can contain other processes, and so on, to any degree of nesting. In the case of processes, some of the responsibilities that cascade down through the fractal structure are the costing, selection, triggering, and evaluation of component processes.

Processes can contain other processes

Of all the resources that processes utilize and generate, the one that seems to cause the most confusion is documentation. A process object is responsible for the conduct of its process, including the generation and verification of any required documentation. The documents themselves, whether paper or electronic, are mechanisms for grouping and recording information about the process. As such, they are information resources, and they exist only to support processes. The following figure shows a few of the documents that might be involved in the purchase of a custom piece of equipment, beginning with the request that creates the purchase object and concluding with a notification that the request has been fulfilled.

Processes may make use of documents

117

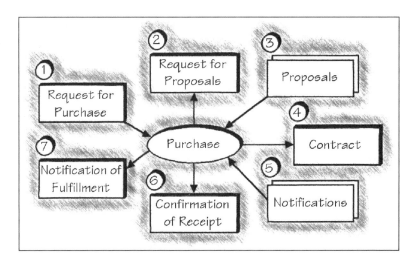

*Processes are
not the same as
documents*

Many work-flow products and "document-centric" interfaces
now on the market confuse processes with documents, using
documents to drive and coordinate organizational processes.
Identifying processes with documents may work for simple processes, but the approach does not scale well to processes that
generate or require multiple documents of varying types.
Moreover, equating processes and documents can lead to systems that resist optimization through the streamlining of documentation. Maintaining a clear distinction between processes
and documents allows a process to use documentation only as
needed, getting rid of documents that bog down the process and
adding others that may improve the process.

*Responsibilities
focus on process
execution*

In order to handle the demands placed on it, a process must be
able to satisfy a wide range of responsibilities. Some typical
responsibilities are shown in the next illustration.

Capabilities of Resources

*Resources
enable and
result from
processes*

Resources enable processes, and resources result from processes.
Resources may be created, destroyed, consumed, reused, owned,
leased, hired, borrowed, contracted, or controlled in other ways.
Given this broad definition, the majority of objects found in a
business model tend to be resource objects. The following figure
entitled "Subclasses of the Resource Class" shows some of the

Process
Initiate activity or resume activity if suspended
Suspend or terminate activity
Add, edit, and delete component processes
Estimate the time and resources required for execution
Accept and report optimization criteria
Execute according to optimization criteria
Select among alternative component processes
Initiate one or more component processes
Report status, schedule, and resource consumption
Request or divest resources as required

major subclasses of Resource, with a few of their subclasses to show how the hierarchy can be extended.

Most of these resources are fairly obvious and familiar to businesspeople. However, conceptual resources are often overlooked despite the fact that they may have tremendous value to the company. Conceptual resources include the corporate mission, its goals and objectives, its plans and programs, and other guiding ideas. Its policies and rules are also important resources, as are its allocation of roles and responsibilities. Capturing these as explicit resources that must be generated and managed can inject meaning into an otherwise lifeless business model.

Conceptual resources are important

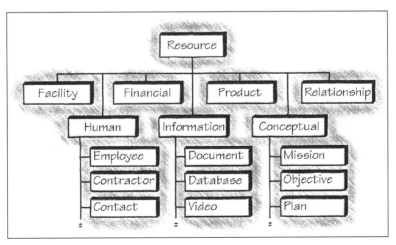

Resources act as virtual inventories

Resource objects act as "virtual inventories" in the sense that processes can assume infinite supplies of resources and not concern themselves with availability. It is up to each resource object to manage its own inventory in a way that meets demand while avoiding excess inventory. Resources track their inventories, current obligations, shipments en route, preferred suppliers, and emergency sources. Based on this information, they make intelligent trade-offs to balance supply against demand. If necessary, a resource object can model the entire supply chain that produces the resource, creating a pull many links deep to ensure timely availability.

Resources schedule their utilization

When a process is asked to schedule itself, it checks its required resources for availability. If the resource objects can supply the requested quantities, they commit these quantities and schedule their delivery. If the process gets commitments for all its required resources, it schedules itself and returns a confirmation. If the process can't get all the resources it needs, it frees the committed resources and fails to schedule as requested. Depending on the urgency of the request, it may then attempt various alternative strategies for getting the resources it needs, including preempting other processes.

Responsibilities focus on utilization

Given the capabilities of resources, they have a rich set of responsibilities. Because there are so many different kinds of resources, these responsibilities will be satisfied in many differ-

Basic structure of a resource.

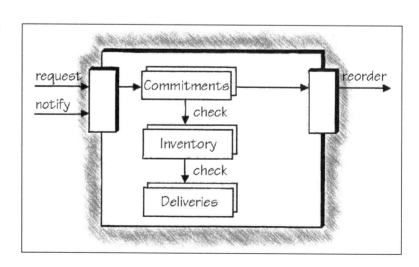

ent ways. But the service interface for the resource class masks these differences, allowing for uniform planning, utilization, and costing. Some key responsibilities of resources objects are shown in the next illustration.

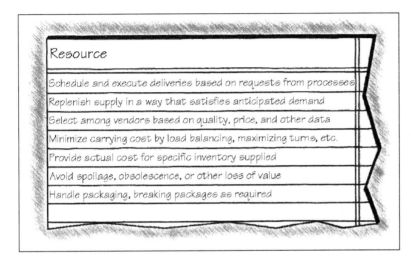

Responsibilities of a resource.

Resource

Schedule and execute deliveries based on requests from processes
Replenish supply in a way that satisfies anticipated demand
Select among vendors based on quality, price, and other data
Minimize carrying cost by load balancing, maximizing turns, etc.
Provide actual cost for specific inventory supplied
Avoid spoilage, obsolescence, or other loss of value
Handle packaging, breaking packages as required

Techniques for Time Management

Although the addition of scheduling and recording adds a powerful new dimension to business objects, these capabilities are easily added to conventional object languages. The simplest approach would be to add scheduling and recording services directly to the BusinessElement class. A better strategy, however, is to delegate these functions to Scheduler and Recorder objects. This not only provides better encapsulation of the time-management functions, it also allows separate class hierarchies of Schedulers and Recorders to be constructed to suit a wide range of needs. Given the separation of responsibilities provided by delegation, each business element is free to use the type of scheduling and recording that works best for it.

Scheduling and recording are easily implemented

Two new classes must be defined to implement scheduling using delegation. The *Scheduler* class manages the schedule and is responsible for making commitments on behalf of a business element. The *Commitment* class holds the information about each individual commitment. Each business element contains its own

Scheduling is handled by Scheduler objects

121

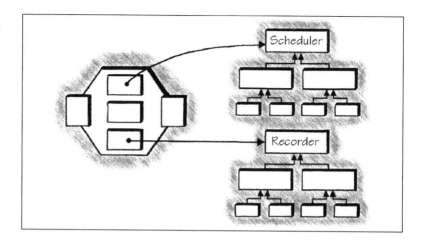

dedicated Scheduler, and the Scheduler may contain any number of Commitments. As the Scheduler takes on new commitments, it generates new Commitment objects and adds these to a time-ordered collection. When the time comes to execute a commitment, the Scheduler sends a message to its parent business element requesting it to carry out the appropriate service. The actual mechanism for triggering the execution of commitments is an implementation detail that depends on the facilities of the language and operating system being used. Most environments provide some form of *event manager* that handles these details transparently.

**A scheduler
object.**

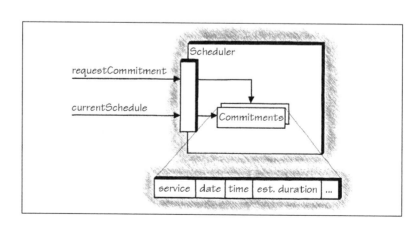

In order to determine whether it can satisfy a requested commitment, a scheduler must have some way of estimating the time required to carry out the action. Depending on the nature of the request, this information can be provided as part of the request, or it can be calculated by the scheduling object. For example, a request to a printing press may include the number of copies required and any special setup requirements. Based on this information, the press can compute the estimated time for the job before allocating that block of time in its schedule.

Commitments require a duration

In many situations, scheduling a business activity requires simultaneous commitments from two or more business elements. In this case, a two-phase commit process may be required for transactions among business elements. In this process, each element involved makes a tentative commitment to schedule itself. The coordinating element then decides if the activity can be carried out effectively given these commitments. If so, it sends messages to all the participating elements to change their commitments to "firm" status. Otherwise, it instructs them to release their tentative commitments and free themselves up for other activities. Although quite simple in nature, this two-phase commit structure lays the foundation for managing complex business transactions, including selling custom manufactured goods and undertaking long-term service contracts.

Commitments may be tentative or firm

As with scheduling, two new classes are required to handle the recording of actions. Each business element contains a single *Recorder,* which generates *Record* objects and places them in a time-ordered collection. The Recorder also provides services for determining when a given action took place, how many times a particular action was executed during a specified time period, and so on. The Recorder may also have methods for automatically archiving records beyond a certain age and for recovering those records if they are required in the future.

Recording is done by Recorder objects

123

The fact that business elements maintain a running record of their actions provides an audit trail for all corporate processes, allowing problems to be diagnosed and corrected. It also provides the quantitative feedback required for sustained process

Recorders facilitate operational auditing

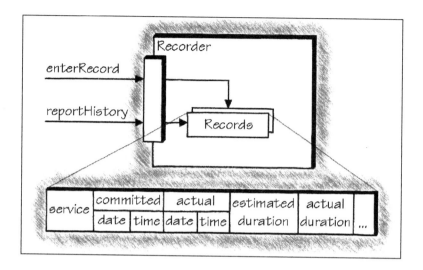

service	committed		actual		estimated	actual	
	date	time	date	time	duration	duration	...

improvement. For example, the information contained in an element's recorder can indicate whether an object is fulfilling its commitments on time. Similarly, a longitudinal comparison of estimated to actual durations can reveal whether cycle times are being reduced according to plan.

8

Optimizing a Business Design

The framework presented in Chapter 7 opens up a world of possibilities for optimizing organizational processes. The current chapter returns to the Dylan example and shows how the design team might take advantage of these possibilities. Some additional techniques for handling roles, relationships, and other design issues are addressed along the way.

Managing Organizations Electronically

Part of the power of organization objects is that they can handle routine management functions such as budgeting, reporting, and requesting approvals. Standard corporate procedures for carrying out these tasks can be defined in the Organization class, then overridden in Division, Department, and other subclasses as required to handle special cases.

Organization objects handle administration

In considering these possibilities, the Dylan design team concludes that the overhead of doing business could be reduced significantly by incorporating administrative processes into the model. Since these costs are currently amortized across all operations, including sales and purchasing, the team decides to broaden the scope of their project to add electronic support for administrative activities.

Administration in Dylan Distributors

125

An informal survey of how Dylan's managers and staff spend their time indicates that the greatest savings can be realized by automating the following administrative activities:

❏ *Budgeting.* This service will be provided by defining and exchanging Budget objects. As shown in the next figure, a Budget object consists of an ordered collection of BudgetLines, each of which has an account category together with dollar amounts for each month in the current fiscal period.

❏ *Spending reporting.* Budget objects will be used for this service as well, except that actual spending will be shown in completed months rather than the budgeted amounts. A SpendingReport object will automatically compare budgeted with actual amounts and display differences, estimate total overruns, and provide other services.

❏ *Activity reporting.* All Process objects used in the Dylan design will have a service for providing management reports that include a description, process owner, period, budget, current status, and other critical information. Organization objects will automatically submit a collection of electronic reports covering all active processes on a weekly basis.

❏ *Activity approval.* For activities that lie beyond the normal scope of an organization or exceed its current spending authority, management reports will be requested from the proposed processes and submitted for approval. These activityApproval objects will have an accession list so that they can automatically move up the chain of authority if the normal approver is unavailable for some reason.

❏ *Spending approval.* Where spending authority is not already covered by a standing budget or an ongoing process, requests for spending approval will be submitted on an as-needed basis. SpendingApprovals will share the accession capabilities of activity approvals via a common Approval superclass.

Many of these activities need to take place on a periodic basis. In these cases, organization objects will hold the activities in their schedules, automatically scheduling the next occurrence each time the current one is completed. For example, Dylan's top management likes to examine its spending reports at the completion of each month. To meet this requirement, the DylanDistributors object will enter this item in its schedule for the first of each month. This entry will initiate requests to all of Dylan's Department objects, triggering an automatic request and rollup of reports as described in the next paragraph. Once the automated reporting is in place, management can easily change the period to weekly reports as well as request current reports at any moment.

Because Organizations are fractal objects, administrative processes such as these are automatically defined for all levels of organization within a company. This feature not only propagates corporate-wide procedures electronically, it also supports the rollup of administrative tasks across levels. For example, the budget for each team goes to its parent department for approval, where it is integrated with budgets for other teams together with the department's own budget, then submitted to the next higher-level organization for approval. Any future restructuring of the company will not disturb these administrative tasks because the rollup of functions is independent of the current corporate structure.

Propagation and rollup are automatic

127

Once the Dylan team has designed in these basic administrative tasks, it realizes it has an excellent opportunity for reuse. Instead of limiting itself to the organizations within the sales, purchas-

Spanning Dylan Distributors

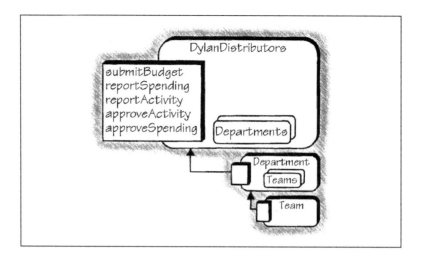

ing, and inventory departments, it adds objects to represent all the other organizations in the company. With this simple extension, it has taken a range of tasks that used to be performed manually or in a variety of spreadsheet and electronic document formats and automated them within the object model. Even though no functional activities are provided for these other departments, many of their administrative tasks will now be handled with no additional effort by the modeling team.

External organizations should be modeled

In addition to representing the internal organization of your own company, it is important to model external organizations and their interactions with your company. This practice is in keeping with the modern concept of the *extended enterprise,* which includes customers, vendors, partners, competitors, financial institutions, regulatory agencies, shareholders, and other interested parties. The practice also creates an infrastructure for tightening relationships with these parties by using electronic communications among objects to accelerate your interactions with them.

128

Beware of subclassing Company

The obvious approach to modeling customers, vendors, and other organizations is to define them as subclasses of a Company class. This approach may be adequate for small-scale systems, but it can lead to some difficult problems in larger deployments. For example, it is quite common for a given company to be both a customer and a vendor. This company is hard to represent if customers and vendors are mutually exclusive subclasses.

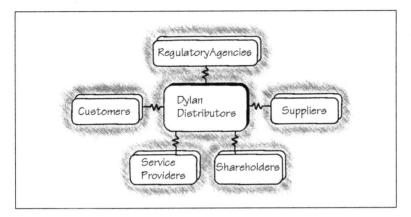

A better tactic is to model outside organizations as subclasses of Organization but represent their relationship to your company using explicit relationship objects. If a company is both a customer and a vendor, it has two distinct relationships. Because these relationships are resources that enable your own sales and purchasing processes, they should be modeled as resources. Interactions with a company in its customer relationship are mediated by a Customer object, and interactions in its vendor relationship are carried out by a Vendor object, as shown below. Each of these relationship objects is attached to the actual company, so requests for services that are independent of the relationship can be passed through to the company itself.

Use relationships to link to other companies

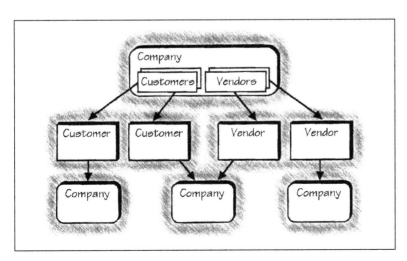

Modeling corporate relationships.

Modeling customers and suppliers

In considering this logic, the Dylan team realizes that it has at least a dozen companies that are both customers and suppliers. It modifies its class hierarchy to add a Relationship class as a subclass of Resource, then moves Customer and Supplier under the Relationship class. In constructing its model, it will create an instance of Organization as well as an instance of one or more relationships for each company it deals with.

First revisions to the Dylan hierarchy.

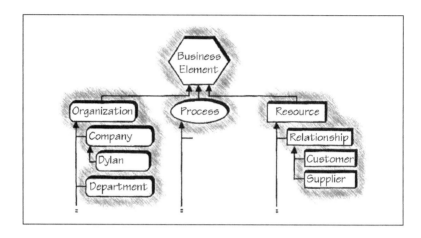

Establishing electronic linkages

As part of rethinking its relationships with other companies, the Dylan team comes up with the idea of forming electronic links to its customers and suppliers. It will do this by providing special interfaces to its software, linking external organizations into its core model using electronic data interchange (EDI). This tight coupling will offer important competitive advantages:

1. Customers will be able to browse the Dylan catalog and place their own orders electronically, making it easier for customers to do business with Dylan. At the same time, this capability will dramatically reduce Dylan's costs of sales because much less human labor will be required.

2. On the supplier side, Dylan will be able to get electronic quotes from suppliers in seconds rather than hours or days, allowing it to further increase the efficiency of its purchasing operations while improving its response time for quoting special orders and out-of-stock products.

Using Processes to Advantage

Process objects are powerful in that they increase the visibility and modifiability of corporate operations. But not all operations should be represented by process objects. Direct messaging between organization and resource objects is simpler, faster, and more efficient. In general, it is the better way to represent basic operations that are relatively stable over time, take the same form in many different processes, and involve a small number of messages.

Use direct messaging for simple interactions

A machine in a work cell, for example, would use direct messages to request the next piece from the machine upstream of it and to ask for any parts it needed to perform its action. There are only a few messages involved, and the form of these messages is the same no matter what the work cell happens to be producing at any given moment. Using process objects for these simple interactions would complicate the model rather than simplify it, so direct messaging is the preferred mechanism.

Collaboration in a work cell

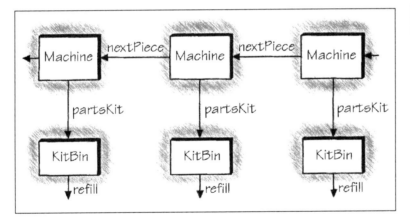

Direct messaging for local interactions.

Where process objects prove their value is with complex sequences of activities that involve multiple objects interacting in unpredictable ways. For example, the flow of activities that begins when a job comes into a manufacturing plant until the finished piece of work is shipped can have many branches and variations. If these different cases appear only as alternative paths through a network of objects, it will be difficult or impossible to trace the flow of events, much less optimize it.

Use process objects for complex interactions

Given this perspective, it will generally be clear when to use process objects instead of direct connections among component objects. When in doubt, review the following checklist. If an activity satisfies any of the following criteria, it is a good candidate for a process object:

❑ *It creates and destroys objects.* Activities that create and destroy the objects that enable them are almost impossible to trace and debug without using explicit process objects.

❑ *It has component activities.* Process objects can contain other processes, which may be generically defined and made available for use by still other processes. It is very difficult to achieve this kind of process reuse with direct messaging.

❑ *It has special cases.* Because a process object is defined by a class, it can be subclassed. This allows general procedures to be defined at a high level and propagated throughout an organization without duplication of effort.

❑ *It requires problem solving.* If an activity requires the use of rules or policies to select its component actions, it should be expressed as a process object to make those decision criteria as visible and modifiable as possible.

❑ *It takes place in "human time."* Activities that take place over spans ranging from minutes to months should be packaged as process objects so that their state can be maintained and monitored by the people involved.

Another way to discover good process objects is to consider the business scenarios developed to drive the design of the business. Instead of capturing "usage" information in a separate analysis tool, this information can be embedded directly in the model. Because the "test cases" for a model are part of the model itself, they are free to evolve over time as the model changes to meet new requirements. Representing this high-level usage information directly in a model is essential to continuous process improvement.

The Dylan team begins its search for process objects by looking at its primary business scenarios, sales, and purchases. Although it was able to represent the sales process as a sequence of collaborations, understanding all the variations in the sales cycle at the

Sale	Process
Create SalesOrder	SalesOrder
Fill in header info.	Customer, SalesOrder
Fill in line items	SalesOrder
Check available stock	InventoryDepartment
Complete SalesOrder	SalesOrder
Request shipment	InventoryDepartment

collaboration level has proved to be a formidable challenge. The team concludes that they have an excellent candidate for a process object. They represent the Sale class, as shown above, ordering the responsibilities according to the overall sequence of events in the case of a simple sale.

Notice that the first thing the Sale process does is create a SalesOrder document to support it. The team considered having this document execute the sales process directly but decided against that approach in order to avoid confounding the roles of processes and documents. Currently, consummating a sale always requires completing a standard sales order. However, the proposed electronic ordering system may require a different kind of document or may not use a document at all. Moreover, special orders may require a purchase order in addition to a sales order. Keeping the sales order separate from the Sale process maintains flexibility while clearly distinguishing between the documents that record information about a process and the process itself.

Preserving the SalesOrder document

One of the goals of the new system is to reduce cycle times on all sales. In order to determine how well this goal is met, the design team decides to instrument the Sale class to monitor its own performance. Each Sale will have a standard cycle time, and it will automatically alert the appropriate Salesperson if that time is exceeded. In addition, a special Recorder is designed for Sale objects that analyzes trends in cycle time and provides a breakdown of how each sale spends its time. The team also decides

Instrumenting the sales process

133

that each Customer will keep a collection of all past Sales and that each Customer object will be responsible for analyzing and reporting Dylan's performance in filling that Customer's needs. Finally, each SalesPerson object will be responsible for collating this information over its own accounts so that the patterns of individual salespeople can be examined to discover opportunities for improvement.

Discovering other processes

Once the Sale class has been roughed out, the Purchase class follows quickly because it is simply the same process viewed from the other side. Probing further, the team discovers several other business activities that deserve promotion to the process level. But the Dylan designers are careful to stop well short of eliminating all direct collaborations among objects. For example, the internal operations of Orders as they generate and roll up their LineItems are left as direct messages because this is the most efficient form.

Using processes to enforce policies

Some of the administrative functions described in the preceding section are promoted to Process objects to make them more visible and modifiable. In the process of making this conversion, the team discovers a trick for defining and "broadcasting" common business policies. For example, there is a corporate spending policy that specifies the required signatures if a manager's authorized level is exceeded. The team decides to represent this policy as a Process object called SpendingApproval and include it as a component of all processes that involve expenditures. With this inclusion, the rules expressed by the services of the SpendingApproval object are automatically checked and approval sought if required. If the company later changes this spending approval policy, a modification to this one object will update all process objects that are affected by the policy.

Optimizing Resource Utilization

Resources may be utilized in four ways

Processes utilize resources in four different ways, as described below and illustrated in the following figure entitled "Four kinds of resource utilization":

1. When a process *consumes* a resource, the resource ceases to have a separate identity.

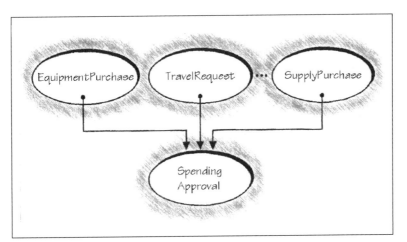

Type of Utilization	Example
Consume	Chemical in a reaction
Incorporate	Part in an assembled product
Monopolize	Machine during a cycle
Access	Information guiding a process

2. When a process *incorporates* a resource, the resource maintains its identity and becomes a component of a composite entity.

3. When a process *monopolizes* a resource, that resource is unavailable to other processes for the duration of the process.

4. When a process *accesses* a resource, the resource remains available to other processes.

135

Utilization patterns vary by industry	Historically, manufacturing has managed its resources in terms of how they are utilized. The primary distinction is between *material* resources, which are either consumed or incorporated in the manufacturing process, and *capacity,* which is the industry term for monopolized resources such as machines and machinists. Service companies rely most heavily on human resources, which are monopolized by processes. The utilities sector sells consumed resources such as gas and electricity, while supporting these with human resources. Finally, information providers deal primarily in accessed resources, although other resources may be consumed or monopolized to provide this access.
The four types block resources to varying degrees	The utilization types shown in the previous figure are ordered in terms of the extent to which they block other processes from using the same resources. Consuming a resource blocks it permanently. Incorporating a resource blocks it permanently unless the resource is recovered by disassembling its composite object. Monopolizing a resource blocks it only for the duration of the process, and accessing a resource typically does not block it at all. Information is one of the few resources that isn't blocked by utilization, which is one of the economic advantages of an information-based organization.
Resource blocking should be minimized	One of the goals of process engineering is to minimize blockage of resources. In the case of consumed and incorporated resources, this means reducing the quantity and cost of resources consumed, including minimizing waste and defects. For monopolized resources, it means reducing the cycle time of the resource so that the resource is available for the next process sooner. Various techniques have been developed in business engineering methodologies for achieving these goals.
Minimizing product costs	The Dylan team examines the resources in its model, looking for each type of utilization in turn. Products are the critical consumed resource in the business. There is not much point in trying to reduce the quantity of products consumed because the company wants to sell as many products as it can, so the emphasis has to be on the costs of its products. Purchasing has already done most of what it can do in terms of negotiating maximum discounts, so the primary effort at pulling cost out of products is directed toward better vendor selection based on current prices and minimizing the carrying costs of inventory. Accordingly, each product is held responsible for monitoring its

own inventory and hitting specific targets for inventory turns, time in storage, and other critical variables. The Inventory-Department is given a scheduled task for reviewing the Inventory on a daily basis and monitoring its overall performance against preset targets.

The most important monopolized resources in the company are personnel and the warehouse facilities. The reduced inventory made possible by the new system should eliminate any bottlenecks on the warehouse side, but there are several measures that can be taken to reduce the load on salespeople and purchasing agents, who account for a significant portion of Dylan's budget. The team estimates that the electronic sales and purchasing assistance built into the new system will reduce cycle times per transaction by about 30 percent, which represents a major savings. Next, the transition to fully electronic processing of routine orders could eliminate human intervention in up to 40 percent of sales and purchases, reducing human cycle times to zero in those cases. Finally, the capabilities built into the sales and purchasing objects should permit less experienced personnel to handle most of the non-electronic orders, allowing average salaries to decrease over time. The net reduction in labor costs for the sales and purchasing functions attributable to the new system is estimated to be close to 60 percent.

Improving capacity utilization

As to the fourth type of utilization, access, the team concludes that the biggest contribution it can make is in the handling of documents. At present, 70 percent of the documents used in Dylan's basic business processes are paper-based. This means that they are a monopolized resource because only one person has access to them at a time, and they often sit idle on people's desks for days at a time. In most cases where Dylan is using electronic documents, it is treating these like paper documents and physically transmitting them from place to place. The team will address the first problem by converting more documents to electronic form in the new system, eliminating paper except for mailed materials with non-electronic orders. It will address the second problem by "publishing" electronic documents in a central database, allowing any number of users to access them simultaneously. This promotes all electronic documents from monopolized resources to accessed resources, reducing their costs and eliminating blocking.

Leveraging information

If every resource is held responsible for knowing how much it costs, actual costing can replace the cruder measures of average or standard costing. Each time a resource is utilized in a process, it reports its cost to the process. The method for computing the cost depends on the type of utilization—consumed or incorporated resources may report their material costs, monopolized resources might charge for their time, and accessed resources could amortize their acquisition cost. All these details are hidden from the process through the use of polymorphism, which simply asks the same question of each resource and rolls up a total cost. In this way, all process objects are capable of actual costing in real time. Not only is actual costing much better than average or standard costing for computing profit, it provides vital feedback to the ongoing effort to optimize resource utilization.

Actual costing for a product rollout.

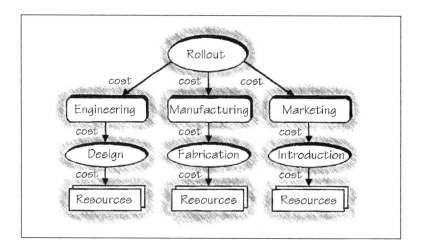

The Dylan design team decides that all resource objects will report their actual costs to the processes that use them. For products, this is relatively easy—each product will retain its purchase cost, including shipping, and add in carrying costs for the time it spends in inventory. Tracking actual labor costs is a bit more challenging. Given that sales and purchasing will be carried out using the electronic assistant screens in the new system, the actual time spent on each order can be tracked. This time is multiplied by the burdened rate for each salesperson and purchasing agent. More generally, the costs of supplies, information acquisition, administrative activities, and other expenses are tracked by the appropriate objects and provided to process objects. The net result is that the new system will help Dylan identify exactly where its costs lie and to compute its actual profits in real time on every single sale.

Managing Human Resources

A critical step in designing any business model is empowering people to play multiple roles. Although the classic view of automation portrayed each person as carrying out a single function, that vision never fit the factory floor very well, and it is even less likely to fit the front office. Almost everyone in an office plays multiple roles, and a system that doesn't support that reality can't adequately represent the workings of the business.

Provide support for multiple roles

The reason that the support for roles is a critical issue is that most object modelers handle job functions by subclassing a generic Employee class by positions such as Manager, Supervisor, and Machinist. This approach works well in the design stage, but it breaks down in the field as soon as the same individual attempts to play more than one role in the company. For example, many manufacturers require that line supervisors maintain their skills by spending a certain percentage of their time working on the production line. In this case, a supervisor could also be a machinist or some other kind of Employee. So which superclass is used? Neither one suffices, and it is hardly practical to switch the object back and forth from one class to another each time the person changes roles.

Don't subclass Employee by position

This problem is directly analogous to the issue of corporate relationships discussed earlier in this chapter. Instead of subclassing Customer off of Company, we subclass Customer off of Relationship, allowing the same company to have multiple relationships. Again, the relationship of being a customer is not the same as the company that bears that relationship. The two must be distinguished because they are very different things.

The problem is analogous to relationships

139

Similarly, Supervisor and Machinist are *roles* that Employees play, not *types* of Employee. Like relationships, these roles are Resources because it is the ability to play useful roles in the company that enables processes. So the Employee on the line who

The same solution applies

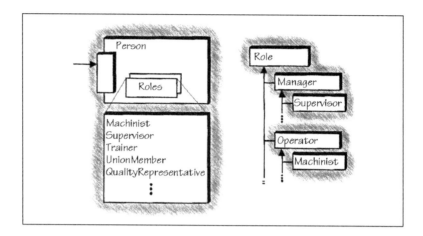

can act either as a supervisor or a machinist is able to play two different roles. Because these roles are subclasses of the Role class, they can be freely assigned to Employees as appropriate, using delegation instead of inheritance to support multiple roles.

Salespeople and supervisors

The Dylan team has stumbled directly into this problem. Senior salespeople are often promoted to sales managers, but they are rarely taken out of the sales role altogether. The same is true with purchasing managers, who continue to manage their established relationships with suppliers. So even though the Dylan team has only two subclasses of Employee in its design, the team is already in trouble. Fortunately, the fix is easy—simply reclassify Salesperson and PurchasingAgent as subclasses of Role, which is a type of Resource. An instance of each of these roles is then attached to the appropriate Person object. The team decides to use Person as the superclass rather than Employee so that any user of the system can be assigned to one or more roles. They are thinking ahead to the day when they can electronically link their customers and suppliers into the system.

People interact through roles

As with relationships and companies, people interact primarily through their roles. If a salesperson needs to have a deal approved by a sales manager, this request goes from the Salesperson object to the SalesManager object, as shown in the following figure. The interaction penetrates through a role object back to a Person object only if a characteristic of the person playing the role is required. For example, the SalesManager role object might check with the

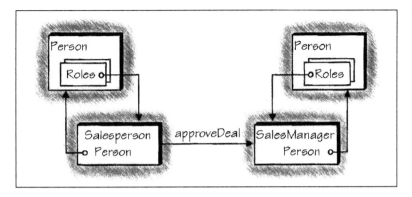

appropriate Person object to see if he or she is on site and able to handle the approval. Scheduling also penetrates through to the Person object. Since a person can only play one role at a time, it is the person who is scheduled rather than the role.

The Dylan Class Hierarchy

Adding the new classes developed in extending their model, Dylan arrives at the hierarchy shown below. The Resource class is the most deeply nested, as is common in business models, so

Extending the hierarchy

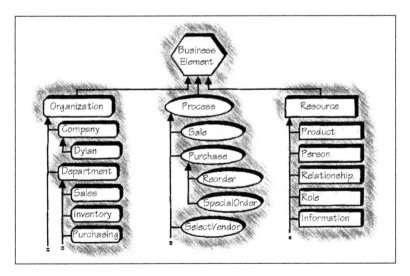

Extension of the Dylan hierarchy.

greater detail is provided on Resource subclasses in the next figure.

Elaborating the Resource class

The Product subclasses appear to be stable in that all products can be classified as Serialized or NonSerialized. As the first figure below suggests, the team has only begun to flesh out the subclasses of Person, Relationship, and Role, so much extension will take place in these classes in the coming months. Finally, the Information class is particularly deep, so it is broken out still further in the second figure below.

The Dylan Resource hierarchy.

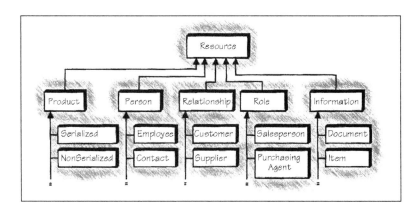

The Dylan Information hierarchy.

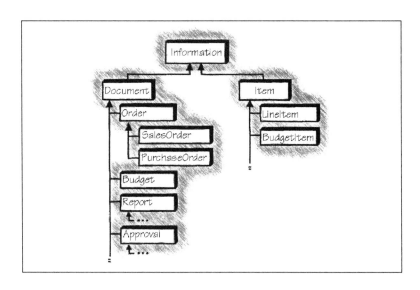

Information will play a key role in Dylan's design, so its sub-classes are already becoming richly elaborated. The primary division is between Documents and Items, where items are components of documents that cannot stand alone. Within documents, there are Orders, Budgets, Reports, Approvals, and many other types, each of which will have numerous subclasses. To date, the team has identified only two types of Items: LineItems and BudgetItems. But the logic of composing documents out of collections of items is highly generic, so many more item types will emerge as the team extends its design.

Elaborating the Information class

A Life Cycle for Convergent Engineering

Even the most powerful convergent model is of no value if it can't be developed, tested, and deployed. The development life cycle that has dominated the industry for many years, the waterfall model, presents developers with a painful dilemma. All the stages of the waterfall are essential to constructing robust systems, yet we can no longer afford the time required for software to wend its way through these stages.

Object-based modeling offers a way out of this dilemma. The solution is to apply the waterfall to every object, from the top-level business model to the most basic component object. The result is a nesting of waterfall cycles that preserves all the benefits of the waterfall approach while greatly accelerating the development process. Using nested waterfalls also offers an unprecedented opportunity to create defect-free software, and it lays a solid foundation for the transition to commercial business components.

Problems with the Waterfall Life Cycle

The prevailing methodology for developing software today is the "waterfall" life cycle, so named because a project cascades through a series of stages from requirements analysis to design, construction, testing, and maintenance. The precise definition of

The waterfall life cycle is the accepted standard

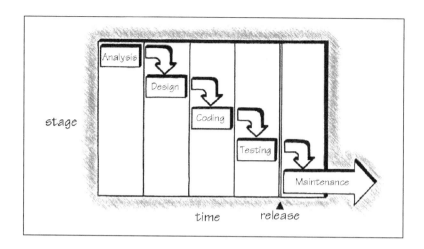

the stages varies from one authority to the next, but the basic pattern is well established.

The waterfall doesn't always flow smoothly

Although the waterfall life cycle is the accepted standard, there is a growing disenchantment with this approach because it rarely works as planned. The various stages are typically initiated in the prescribed sequence, but they are rarely completed in the manner shown. In many cases, new requirements continue to be generated well into final testing, requiring constant redesign and reworking of completed code. These shifting requirements undermine the entire life cycle, resulting in software that is chronically late, over budget, and plagued by defects. Although developers and management inevitably blame each other for these failures, the real problem lies in the failure of the monolithic application to meet constantly changing business needs.

Rapid prototyping is one alternative

Many developers using object technology have abandoned the conventional waterfall in favor of an approach known as *rapid prototyping*. In this technique, developers translate requests for functionality directly into code, then show the results to managers to get their feedback. This process is iterated in short cycle times until an agreeable solution is reached.

Rapid prototyping doesn't scale well

Although rapid prototyping has yielded spectacular results with programs created by a single individual or a small team, it would form a weak foundation for the development of corporate systems involving hundreds of developers. It is simply not possible

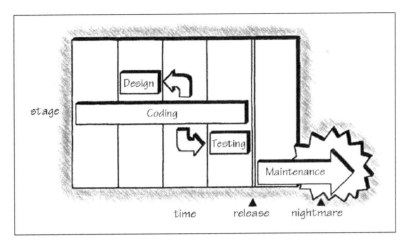

to dive right into the coding process and produce large-scale, maintainable business systems. Attempts to do so more often lead to a process more appropriately characterized as *rabid prototyping,* as illustrated above.

Despite its shortcomings, it's impossible to dismiss the waterfall methodology because all of its stages are essential. Good analysis, careful design, and rigorous testing are essential ingredients of robust business systems. Skip any of these stages and these systems will be (1) irrelevant to the needs of the business, (2) so poorly structured that they don't perform their intended tasks, (3) riddled with so many bugs that they fail to work reliably, or (4) all of the above.

All of the waterfall stages are essential

At present, most efforts to develop an improved software methodology involve retaining the stages of the waterfall cycle but using multiple passes through the first four stages to produce a deliverable system. In both the *iterative* and the *spiral* approaches, the first pass through the waterfall produces a simplified version of the target system. Successive passes add functionality and detail, using feedback from earlier passes to guide the development of the system. These variations of the waterfall have met with mixed success. They do help break down multiyear projects into smaller, more manageable units. But they don't decompose projects in a way that allows for simultaneous development efforts. They simply replace one big waterfall with a string of successive waterfalls.

Variations on the waterfall are being explored

147

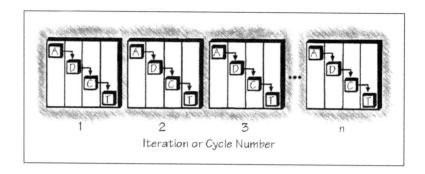

Iteration or Cycle Number

Adapting the Waterfall to Model-Based Systems

Model-based systems decompose the effort

Model-based systems suggest a new variant on the waterfall life cycle that does a better job of decomposing a project into independent development efforts. The formula is simple: Remove analysis as a separate stage, then apply the waterfall life cycle to every object in a system.

Nested waterfalls simplify development

A convergent engineering project begins with the modeling of a high-level business element, which may be an organization, process, or resource. The design of that element identifies and sets the requirements for a number of component objects. If these objects are well designed, their implementations will be independent of each other and can all be developed simultaneously. The design of these component objects will, in turn, identify the need for still lower level objects, each of which can be developed independently, and so on. Naturally, developers should seek opportunities for reuse at every level. If an object has already been designed, constructed, and tested, it should be reused rather than reinvented.

148

Constructing the Dylan system

Dylan Distributors uses nested waterfalls to construct its new system. The top object, DylanDistributors, is broken down into Department objects—Sales, Inventory, Purchasing, and other departments that are included for integrating routine administrative tasks. Each Department object is composed of other objects such as Customer, Salesperson, Product, and so on. This design decomposition cascades down the levels until base-level objects are reached.

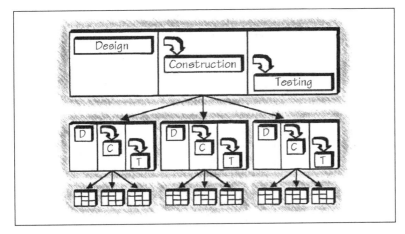

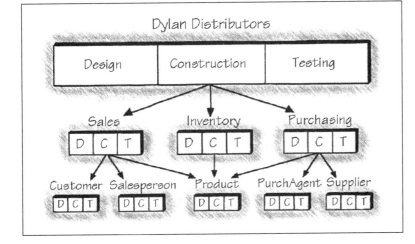

When the decomposition process reaches base-level objects, which have no component objects, these base-level objects are designed, constructed, and tested. They are then passed up to the next higher level, where they are combined and subjected to integration testing. This rollup continues until the top-level object has been assembled and tested.

Rollup is mostly integration testing

This nested waterfall life cycle is another example of fractal patterns at work. What the methodology does is perform a fractal decomposition of a development project. The following figure shows the nested waterfall methodology in a way that not only

This development life cycle is fractal

149

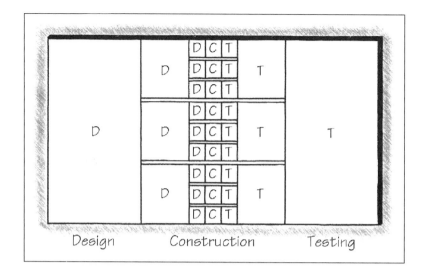

Design   Construction   Testing

makes the fractal nature more apparent but also shows more clearly the support for parallel development activities. This form also illustrates the common observation that the larger a system, the greater proportion of time that is spent in design and testing.

This approach requires discipline

Nesting development cycles is the key to leveraging the proven advantages of the waterfall methodology while avoiding its known liabilities. It requires discipline, however, to apply the method at every level. Particularly as developers get down to base-level objects, they will be tempted to just figure out what they want and start generating code. But the waterfall is appropriate even at the level of base objects. The stages may be executed very quickly, but each one of them is essential.

Following the life cycle must not be a burden

Because the waterfall life cycle is so well established in most organizations, it is often encumbered with heavy documentation and approval requirements that would bring a fast-paced object-modeling project to an abrupt halt. It is important to remember that the administrative aspects of the waterfall life cycle were intended for large-scale applications and do not apply to the micro-level development efforts involved in convergent engineering. Although the waterfall itself is preserved, most of the policies and procedures surrounding it must be greatly streamlined to apply the waterfall in this context.

Advantages of Analysis by Design

The reason there is no formal requirements analysis in this version of the waterfall life cycle is that the requirements for each object are specified by the design at the level above, as shown below. For example, the design of a FabricationPlant object determines what the WorkCenter, LoadingDock, Inventory, and other component objects must do to fulfill their roles. The design process specifies the services that these objects will provide and the object interfaces by which the services will be invoked. If each component object provides the required services and carries out its other assigned responsibilities, it will have met its requirements. So the components do not need requirements analysis. They proceed directly to the design stage. The same is true of their components, and so on.

Requirements cascade down the levels

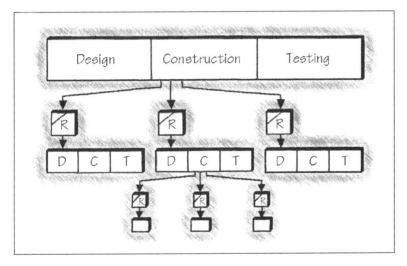

Cascading requirements.

This cascading works for every level of a system except the top one, which has no higher level to set its requirements. In this case, there may be a need for a separate analysis activity. Of course, this is the most important case because the top-level design drives all the others. But even here, there are good reasons for not defining a separate analysis phase.

The top-level object is the exception

151

The role of analysis in conventional application development is to specify precisely the requirements of a completed application. Given that applications are problem-oriented by nature, this

Conventional analysis is problem-based

analysis process ensures that the application will actually solve the problem at hand. In this context, completing analysis before beginning design is essential to producing effective solutions.

Convergent engineering analyzes the business

But model-based systems aren't built to solve individual problems—they are intended to represent the workings of a business in a way that reflects the critical activities of that business. So the role of analysis is to understand the business itself, not a particular problem within that business. While it is possible to analyze a business in abstract terms, this often turns out to be an unproductive exercise. Building a working model has proved to be an excellent vehicle for gaining consensus on how a business works because defining and naming the components of the model and their interactions requires explicit agreement on what is represented by these components and interactions. This process, which is shown graphically below, is known as *analysis by design.*

Opportunities enriching a design.

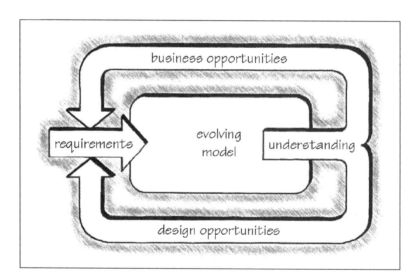

152 *Object advantages become evident earlier*

Another reason for combining analysis and design is that the advantages of object technology can be applied earlier and more effectively. Thinking in terms of objects and their relationships causes managers to view their businesses in new ways that often lead to important insights. Couching analysis in the context of an object-based modeling activity almost always suggests opportunities for improving a system that would never have been conceived if requirements were determined prior to starting design work.

Building Defect-Free Systems

The advent of object technology is often depicted as a second Industrial Revolution. The basic concept behind this analogy is that software construction, like the fabrication of material goods 100 years ago, is shifting from unique, hand-crafted products to rapidly assembled systems built out of standard reusable components. In the case of this new Industrial Revolution, the products are software systems and the standard, reusable components are objects.

Object assembly invites a revolution in software

The shift to software by assembly has major advantages, including reduced costs, faster construction time, and increased quality. The reduced costs and faster construction stem from the fact that much less work is done for any given system—the primary effort consists of assembling existing components into a new configuration. The increased quality results from the reuse of components that have already been debugged and refined in previous software systems.

Object technology enhances quality

Although the reuse of existing components provides a much needed boost to software quality, there is much more that could be done in this area. The control of quality in the conventional waterfall relies primarily on a final testing stage to catch any defects in a system and remove them prior to delivery. This is how manufacturers approached quality up until about 15 years ago, prior to the advent of just-in-time (JIT) manufacturing and its zero-defects credo.

Further increases in quality are possible

Old-style manufacturing, like contemporary software development, was geared to keeping the process moving forward and on schedule. If defective components were detected during the manufacturing process, they were either reworked or scrapped. To ensure adequate quality, random samples of completed products were pulled off the end of the line and tested. Statistical techniques were used to generalize from the sample to ensure that an adequate percentage of products being shipped to customers was free of defects.

Manufacturers used to control defects

This approach to quality is now considered inadequate by modern manufacturers. The problem is that the approach virtually guarantees that a known percentage of defective products is

They now strive to eliminate defects

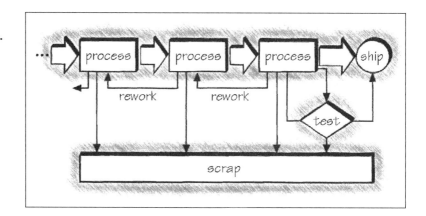

being placed in the hands of customers. The modern approach to quality, as pioneered by Japanese auto manufacturers, is to strive to eliminate defects altogether.

The zero-defects approach concentrates on process

The key to turning out consistently defect-free products is to focus not on the products themselves but on the processes that create them. In a JIT manufacturing facility, every operator has access to a red cord or switch that halts the entire production line. Whenever an operator discovers a defect, he or she immediately shuts down the line. All the operators assemble as a team to figure out how the defect occurred, then modify their processes to ensure that this type of defect never occurs again. The results of this new approach have been so successful that the zero-defects approach is now embraced by virtually every modern manufacturer.

Software should also be defect-free

If software construction is to be modeled after the manufacturing process, the contemporary approach to manufacturing quality should serve as the paradigm for software quality. Instead of attempting to test out defects at the end of the development process, software developers should build in quality at every step of the process. Only in this way can the next generation of software provide robustness and quality while remaining open to constant evolution and adaptation.

154

Wacker Siltronic

Although the goal of defect-free software may seem ambitious, it is now a proven option. Several years ago, Wacker Siltronic, a manufacturer of silicon wafers, used this approach to build a new, object-oriented oven-control system for mixing and baking

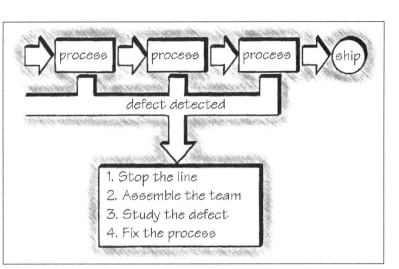

silicon. Four defects were discovered during development, and four more were discovered during final testing. In each case, appropriate process changes were made. The final product has been in service 24 hours a day for more than three years at the time of this writing, and it has yet to exhibit a single defect. Moreover, the system has been revised and enhanced extensively during that time, and not one of these modifications has introduced a defect.

A further advantage of the nested waterfall is that it allows rigorous unit testing to take place on many levels. At each level, the design for an object should be thoroughly tested for consistency, completeness, and other critical properties before being released as a specification for constructing its component objects. When the component objects have been returned, they should be assembled and subjected to integration testing, limits testing, stress testing, and all the other tests normally applied to high-level systems.

The nested waterfall can enhance quality further

155

Testing individual components prior to integrating them into larger systems is know as *unit* testing. Unit testing has long proved its value in reducing software defects because it is possible to test for all the possible sources of errors with smaller units of software. Given that objects function as self-contained, independent models of business elements, objects are ideal subjects for unit testing. Applied consistently, rigorous unit testing of

Unit testing takes place at every level

every object at every level provides a solid foundation for developing defect-free software.

Optimization through Simulation

The goal is convergent quality

Of course, a system can be totally free of defects on the software level and still miss the mark in business terms. Once again, the goal of convergent engineering is to design and construct a model that integrates the business and its supporting software. The quality of this integrated system must extend all the way from the lowest-level method to the highest-level business process. In this larger sense, quality implies more than the absence of defects. It means conducting the business as efficiently and effectively as possible.

Simulation is a powerful engineering tool

Testing for business quality requires an entirely new set of techniques. The capacity for simulation offers a singularly powerful tool for this purpose. At any time during the development process, one or more models can be tested with sample inputs to see how well they handle a test suite of business situations. You can debug business processes, examine corporate performance under varying conditions of load and capacity, extrapolate the effects of organizational changes, or explore new areas of business to see how your company might fare.

Use simulation throughout development

It's never too soon to begin simulating business processes. In the convergent engineering approach, informal simulation begins the very first time a business design team does the first talk-through with its class cards. Actual software simulations should be run as soon as the design of the top-level model is complete, using placeholder objects to "stub out" lower-level functions. This technique allows improvements in the overall design before construction begins at the deeper levels.

Test the model under actual business conditions

A very effective strategy is to prototype user interface screens in parallel with the initial modeling effort so that the performance of the business system can be tested with real employees as early as possible. These tests should be conducted systematically and scientifically, simulating real-world situations very closely and extracting detailed performance measures for speed, accuracy, and overall effectiveness. The results of these tests can lead

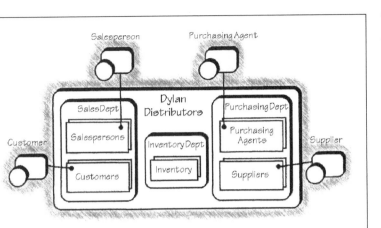

to major enhancements to the model, many of which will be
suggested by the future operators of the system. The above figure shows the high-level Dylan model being tested in a form
that includes real-time electronic interactions with customers and
suppliers.

Because all objects can perform actual costing, your simulations
can provide immediate feedback on how any combination of
changes will affect your costs and profits. If you discover a
change that looks as if it should improve the business, you can
roll that change right back into the operational version of the
model because the operational system and the offline simulator
are just two different uses of the same system. Assuming you
have designed your objects to be self-monitoring, you can get
rapid feedback on whether your actual results match the predictions of your simulation. You can then use this feedback to
improve your model to enhance both its real-time performance
as well as its simulation accuracy.

*Financial effects
are directly
measurable*

In addition to manual simulations, in which you personally
make changes to your business design and then run the model to
see how well they work, you should design in the capacity for
automated simulation. With this type of simulation, an offline
copy of the operational system may run for many hours unat-
tended, exploring parametric variations in operating characteristics. The parameters to explore can range from the number of
service representatives available at different hours of the day to

*Automated
simulation is
ongoing*

157

the effects of different rate structures on shipping costs. Using standard goal-seeking techniques known as *hill-climbing algorithms,* the model can examine the simultaneous effects of varying many parameters at once, automatically homing in on the most profitable alternative.

Constant simulation is cost-effective

These simulations are time-consuming, but they can run as background tasks that never steal computing cycles from the operational version of the model. Moreover, the simulations offer an excellent use of otherwise wasted computing power during the 12 to 16 hours a day that most machines sit idle. What better way to leverage your investment in hardware and software than having it work all night figuring out how to make your company more profitable?

Toward Software by Assembly

The future belongs to commercial components

The discussion up to this point has tacitly assumed that all objects are designed and created in house because that is today's reality. But eventually, an open market for business components will emerge, and we will begin to make the transition from scratch-built systems to software by assembly. Which raises one final question—what will be the methodology for software by assembly?

The goal is self-assembling components

The dream is that we can just snap software components from multiple vendors together and they will fit perfectly the first time. If this were truly possible, we wouldn't need a methodology for software by assembly—we'd just need a few instructions of the "insert Tab A in Slot B" variety. Any minor incompatibilities among the components would be worked out among themselves.

Until then, we need a methodology

Perhaps a day will come when this dream is realized. In the foreseeable future, we are going to have to deal with manual assembly, compatibility problems, workarounds, custom components, and a host of other issues that will require a systematic methodology even in the age of software by assembly.

The nested waterfall will do the job

The nested waterfall life cycle is an excellent vehicle for that methodology. There is nothing in the approach that requires all components to be built from scratch. In fact, the methodology

158

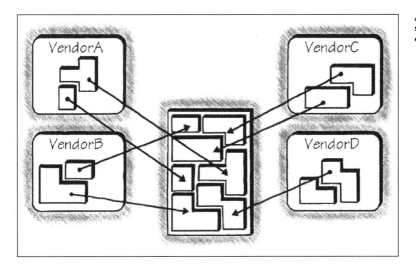

encourages reuse at every level. The major focus is on the design of systems and the integration of components. Purchased components can be plugged into a design at any level with no effect on the methodology except a reduction in work.

This means that the nested waterfall life cycle offers a smooth migration path to the future of software by assembly. It works today in an environment in which every object is constructed from scratch. As generic business objects become available, it will embrace them. And if the time should come when objects are able to assemble themselves, it will still provide a common framework to support these objects and facilitate their connections. The fractal structure may well be the software architecture of the future.

It offers a smooth path to the future

If you made it this far, I have accomplished my goal. I have constructed in your mind a working model of how business and software can be integrated to amplify the abilities of both. Even if you disagree with the ideas I have expressed here, you will think a little differently for having considered them, and some part of your mind will continue to wrestle with the problems I have posed and the solutions I've suggested. If the sales of my previous books are any indication, there will soon be tens of thousands of you working in parallel on these issues, which begins to tap the kind of power we will need to change the way people think about organizations, information systems, and the potential synergy between the two.

Of course, you may have fooled me and started at the back of the book. In that case, I can only say that I admire your creativity and wish you well in your attempt to reconstruct the logic of the book as you wend your way backwards to the Foreword.

Regardless of how you arrived at this page, let me close with an invitation. My company publishes a newsletter called Enterprising Objects. *This is our vehicle for sustaining the dialog that will be required to define a common semantics for business objects and bring about an open market for reusable business components. If you are interested in learning more about the newsletter, are curious about our company, or want to offer some feedback on this book, please contact us. We look forward to hearing from you.*

Enterprise Engines Inc.
999 Baker Way, Suite 400
San Mateo, CA 94404
Voice: (415) 525-1900
Fax: (415) 525-2828
Internet: enterprise@engines.com

Class Cards for the Dylan Model

The following pages provide a snapshot of the Dylan design at the end of the design session described in Chapter 5. This is the form in which the cards are used for walk-throughs. Subsequent detailing, as described in Chapter 6, moves common responsibilities into abstract superclasses and also increases the degree of encapsulation by routing messages between departments through the appropriate Department classes. None of the extensions to the design described in Part 3 are included on these cards.

The Dylan class hierarchy reflected in these cards is as follows. The four abstract classes, which were not yet created at the end of Chapter 5, are identified in italics and are listed only to provide structure for the concrete classes. The cards for the concrete classes are presented in the order shown.

Company
    DylanDistributors
    Customer
    Supplier
Department
    SalesDepartment
    InventoryDepartment
    PurchasingDepartment

Employee
  Salesperson
  PurchasingAgent
Product
Order
  SalesOrder
  PurchaseOrder
LineItem

DylanDistributors CLASS	Company SUPERCLASS
RESPONSIBILITIES	COLLABORATORS
Add/edit/remove a Department	Departments, Department
Handle incoming Customer calls	SalesDepartment
Departments[ ]	COMPONENTS

Add/edit/remove a Department:
> Request that the Departments collection add, remove, or
> look up a Department.
> In the edit case, request that the indicated Department edit
> itself.

Handle incoming customer calls:
> Delegate the responsibility for these customer calls by
> requesting that the SalesDepartment handle the call.

Customer	CLASS	Company	SUPERCLASS
Know name, addresses, etc.	RESPONSIBILITIES		COLLABORATORS
Know assigned Salesperson			
Know discount schedule			
Know balance & payment status		Customers	
Issue statements		Customers	
Collect past-due amounts		Customers	
Record/report history of sales		SalesHistory, Customers	
Project sales by Products		Customers	
Customers[ ]—Optional fractal component Customers			COMPONENTS
SalesHistory [SalesOrder]—Collection of filled sales orders			

Know name, address, salesperson, etc.:
This is a catch-all responsibility to maintain all the object's basic information.

Know assigned SalesPerson:
Accept or report the SalesPerson assigned to this Customer.

Know discount schedule:
Use a discounting algorithm to provide a discount on each sale.

Apply or report any product-specific discounts for this customer.

Know balance and payment status:
Track and report current balance owed by customer.

Report whether customer is current, late, or delinquent in payment.

Issue statements:
Request Accounting System to issue a statement as required.

Collect past-due amounts:
Track average payment date for this customer.

Issue dunning letters and calls if payment status is late.

Transfer to collections agency if status goes to delinquency.

Record/report history of sales:
Analyze buying patterns in SalesHistory and display graphic breakdown and trends.

Project sales by products:
Use statistical forecasting techniques to estimate future sales.

Provide results by product and/or total, volume and/or dollar amount.

Apply seasonal adjustment algorithms as appropriate.

Supplier	CLASS	Company	SUPERCLASS
Know name, addresses, etc.	RESPONSIBILITIES		COLLABORATORS
Know discount schedule		Product	
Supply product & price information		Catalog, Product	
Quote a quantity of a Product		Catalog, Product	
Record/report history of purchases		PurchaseHistory	
Catalog[Product]—Listing & prices of products offered by this supplier		COMPONENTS	
PurchaseHistory[PurchaseOrder]—All prior purchases from this supplier			

Know name, address, etc.:
> This is a catch-all responsibility to maintain all the object's basic information.

Know discount schedule:
> Use a discounting algorithm to estimate a discount on each purchase.
>
> Record or report Product-specific discounts offered by this Supplier.

Supply product & price information:
> Look up a Product in the Catalog.
>
> Request that a Product supply its description and price list.

Quote a quantity of a product:
> Request that a Product provide its quantity discount price.

Record/report history of purchases:
> Analyze buying patterns in PurchaseHistory and display graphic breakdown and trends.

SalesDepartment CLASS	Department SUPERCLASS
RESPONSIBILITIES Add/edit/remove a Salesperson	Salespeople COLLABORATORS
Add/edit/remove a Customer	Customers
Add/edit/remove available Product	Catalog
Route an incoming call	Customers, Customer, Salesperson
Forecast demand by Product	Customers, Customer
Salespeople[ ] COMPONENTS	
Customers[ ]—All active customers of Dylan Distributors	
Catalog[Product]—Listing & prices of all available products	

Add/edit/remove a Salesperson:
> Request that the Salespeople collection add, remove, or look up a Salesperson.
>
> In the edit case, request that the indicated Salesperson edit itself.

Add/edit/remove a Customer:
> Request that the Customers collection add, remove, or look up a Customer.
>
> In the edit case, request that the indicated Customer edit itself.

Add/edit/remove a Product:
> Request that the Products collection add, remove, or look up a Product.
>
> In the edit case, request that the indicated Product edit itself.

Route an Incoming call:
> If needed, look up Customer in the Customers collection.
> Ask Customer to supply identity of assigned Salesperson.
> Send message to Salesperson to accept call.

Forecast demand by product:
> Request each Customer to project sales to it of the specified product.
> Total these forecasts and return the count and dollar amount.

Inventory- Department	CLASS	Department	SUPERCLASS
Report stock for a Product	RESPONSIBILITIES	Inventory, Product	COLLABORATORS
Ship Products to Customers		SalesOrder, Customer, Inventory, Product	
Accept Products from Suppliers		PurchaseOrder, Supplier, Inventory, Product	
Inventory[Product]—Products currently available for shipment	COMPONENTS		

Report stock for a Product:
> If needed, look up Product in the Inventory collection.
> Request from Product its current stock level.

Ship Products to Customers:
> If needed, look up Product in the Inventory collection.
> Ask Product to supply desired quantity.

Accept Products from Suppliers:
> If needed, look up Product in the Inventory collection.
> Ask Product to accept shipment.

Purchasing-Department	CLASS	Department	SUPERCLASS
RESPONSIBILITIES		**COLLABORATORS**	
Add/edit/remove a PurchasingAgent		PurchasingAgents, PurchasingAgent	
Add/edit/remove a Supplier		Suppliers, Supplier	
Submit a PurchaseOrder		Suppliers, PurchasingAgents, PurchasingAgent	
Suppliers[ ]—All suppliers used by Dylan		**COMPONENTS**	
PurchasingAgents[ ]			

Add/edit/remove a PurchasingAgent:

Ask the PurchasingAgents collection to add, remove, or look up a PurchasingAgent.

In the edit case, request that the indicated PurchasingAgent edit itself.

Add/edit/remove a Supplier:

Ask the Suppliers collection to add, remove, or look up a Supplier.

In the edit case, request that the indicated Supplier edit itself.

Submit a PurchaseOrder:

Accept product and quantity information from Product object.

Select best Supplier based on quality, price, and fulfillment time.

Select a PurchasingAgent to handle the order.

Ask PurchasingAgent to submit the PurchaseOrder.

Salesperson	CLASS	Employee	SUPERCLASS
RESPONSIBILITIES			**COLLABORATORS**
Add/edit/remove a Customer		Accounts	
Accept/initiate a sales call		Accounts, Customer	
Create/complete a SalesOrder		SalesOrder	
Verify inventory		InventoryDepartment	
Request shipment		InventoryDepartment	
Accounts[Customer]—Customers assigned to this Salesperson			**COMPONENTS**

Add/edit/remove a Customer:
Ask the Accounts collection to add, remove, or look up a Customer.

In the edit case, request that the indicated Customer edit itself.

Accept/initiate a sales call:
If needed, look up the Customer in the Accounts collection.

Bring up Sales screen with history and action tools.

Supply screen with appropriate Customer information.

Wait for Salesperson to click ACCEPTCALL or PLACECALL.

If no reply, take a message or turn call over to another Salesperson.

Create/complete a SalesOrder:
Create a new instance of SalesOrder.

Ask the new SalesOrder to fill itself in.

Verify inventory:
Request stock levels for Product from InventoryDepartment.

Request shipment:
Ask InventoryDepartment to ship ordered Product.

PurchasingAgent CLASS	Employee SUPERCLASS
RESPONSIBILITIES	COLLABORATORS
Initiate/accept a purchase call	Supplier
Create/complete a PurchaseOrder	PurchaseOrder

Suppliers [ ]—Suppliers this Purchasing Agent deals with   COMPONENTS

Add/edit/remove a Supplier:
Ask the Accounts collection to add, remove, or look up a Supplier.

In the edit case, request that the indicated Supplier edit itself.

Accept/initiate a purchase call:
Look up the Supplier in the Suppliers collection.

Bring up Purchasing screen with history and action tools.

Fill screen with appropriate supplier information.

Wait for purchasing agent to click ACCEPTCALL or PLACECALL.

If no reply, take a message or turn call over to another agent.

Create/complete a PurchaseOrder:
Create an instance of PurchaseOrder.

Ask the new PurchaseOrder to fill itself in.

Product	CLASS		SUPERCLASS
RESPONSIBILITIES		COLLABORATORS	
Know name, description, etc.			
Know current stock level			
Know price and discount			
Know actual cost			
Report quantity discounted price			
Forecast demand & optimize stock		SalesDepartment	
Reorder as required		PurchasingDepartment	
		COMPONENTS	

Know name, description, etc.:
> This is a catch-all responsibility to maintain all the object's basic information.

Know current stock level:
> Add to, remove from, or report current stock level.

Know price and discount:
> Accept, compute, or report the current price and the current discount.

Know actual cost:
> Track and report cost of each product individually or by batch.

Report quantity discounted price:
> Apply quantity discount to the supplied quantity and return the extended price.

Forecast demand & optimize stock:
> Ask SalesDepartment to forecast demand for this product.
> Look up or compute carry costs per unit of inventory.
> Calculate the minimum quantity to meet demand.
> Add additional stock for inventory against unexpected orders.

Reorder as required:
> Compute economic order quantity (EOC) based on current discounts.
> Request a purchase action from PurchasingDepartment.

SalesOrder	CLASS	Order	SUPERCLASS
Fill in header information RESPONSIBILITIES		Customer	COLLABORATORS
Add/edit/remove LineItem		LineItems	
Fill in footer information		LineItems, LineItem, Customer	
Display/print order form			
LineItems [ ]			COMPONENTS

Fill in header information:

Request name, shipping address, and other information from Customer.

Enter this information in the appropriate fields of electronic order form.

Enter the current date, freezing this date when order is confirmed.

Add/edit/remove a LineItem:

Ask the LineItems collection to add, remove, or look up a LineItem.

In the edit case, request that the indicated LineItem edit itself.

Fill in footer information:

Request non-product-specific discount schedule from Customer.

Poll LineItems for extended prices, discounts, and taxable amounts.

Compute total of each and factor in Customer discount.

Add shipping and other costs to finalize SalesOrder.

Display/print order form:

Display/print header information at top of form.

Ask each LineItem to display/print itself in body of form.

Display/print footer information at bottom of form.

PurchaseOrder	CLASS	Order	SUPERCLASS
Fill in header information	RESPONSIBILITIES	Supplier	COLLABORATORS
Add/edit/remove LineItem		LineItems	
Display/print order form			
Report total price		LineItems, LineItem, Supplier	
LineItems[ ]			COMPONENTS

Fill in header information:

Request name, order address, and other information from Supplier.

Enter this information in the appropriate fields of electronic order form.

Enter the current date, freezing this date when order is sent.

Add/edit/remove a LineItem:

Request that the LineItems collection add, remove, or look up a LineItem.

In the edit case, request that the indicated LineItem edit itself.

Display/print order form:

Display/print header information at top of form.

Request each LineItem to display/print itself in body of form.

Report total price:

For all LineItems in the LineItems collection, request their price and keep a running total.

Ask the Supplier to report its discount factor and apply it to the total price.

Business Engineering

The first suggested reading is Fredrick Taylor's classic text on "scientific management," which is arguably the progenitor of all business engineering efforts. The next five books, by Peters, Drucker, Ohmae, Davis, and Savage, provide a cross section of current thinking on the problems of management in the new age of global competition and accelerating change. The remaining texts offer a rich variety of ideas, objectives, and techniques for the corporate reengineering process.

Fredrick Winslow Taylor, *Scientific Management*, New York: Harper, 1911.

Tom Peters, *Thriving on Chaos: Handbook for a Management Revolution*, New York: Knopf, 1987.

Peter F. Drucker, *The New Realities*, New York: Harper & Row, 1989.

Kenichi Ohmae, *The Borderless World: Power and Strategy in the Interlinked Economy*, New York: HarperCollins, 1990.

Stanley M. Davis, *Future Perfect*, Reading, MA: Addison-Wesley, 1987.

Charles A. Savage, *Fifth Generation Management: Integrating Enterprises through Human Networking*, Digital Press, 1990.

Michael Hammer and James Champy, *Reengineering the Corporation: A Manifesto for Business Revolution*, New York: HarperCollins, 1993.

H. J. Harrington, *Business Process Improvement: The Breakthrough Strategy for Total Quality, Productivity and Competitiveness*, New York: McGraw-Hill, 1991.

Philip R. Thomas, *Competitiveness through Total Cycle Time: An Overview for CEOs,* New York: McGraw-Hill, 1990.

Geary A. Rummler and Alan P. Brache, *Improving Performance: How to Manage the White Space on the Organization Chart,* San Francisco: Jossey-Bass Publishers, 1990.

Anthony Crawford, *Advancing Business Concepts in a JAD Workshop Setting: Business Reengineering and Process Redesign,* Englewood Cliffs, NJ: Yourdon Press, 1994.

Supporting Technologies

This section of readings deals with the use of technology to meet the new business challenges. The first two books, by Keen and Quinn, provide excellent overviews with many important insights. The other books flesh out some of the promise and problems with applying information technology to business engineering. The Business Week *article reports the study showing that information technology must be integrated with business engineering if the technology is going to have any payoff to the organization.*

Peter G. W. Keen, *Shaping the Future: Busines Design through Information Technology,* Boston: Harvard Business School Press, 1991.

James Brian Quinn, *Intelligent Enterprise: A Knowledge and Service Based Paradigm for Industry,* New York: Free Press, 1992.

Don Tapscott and Art Caston, *Paradigm Shift: The New Promise of Information Technology,* New York: McGraw-Hill, 1993.

Thomas H. Davenport, *Process Innovation: Reegineering Work through Information Technology,* Boston: Harvard Business School Press, 1993.

Robert Johansen, *Groupware: Computer Support for Business Teams,* New York: The Free Press (Macmillan), 1988.

William H. Davidow and Michael S. Malone, *The Virtual Corporation,* New York: HarperCollins, 1992.

Howard Gleckman et al., "The Technology Payoff," *Business Week,* June 14, 1993, pp. 57–68.

Object Technology

The following readings provide more insight into the tools and techniques of object technology. The first two books on the list are geared toward managers and use the same format and presentation style of the present work. The third book, by Khoshafian et al., is one of the few texts to adequately address the business benefits of object technology and offers a tantalizing preview of the future of organizations. Harmon and Taylor provide a collection of real-world examples of object technology being applied to business problems, including the Wacker Siltronic project described in Chapter 9. The remaining books provide techniques for object-oriented analysis and design. Foremost among these, in my opinion, is Wirfs-Brock et al.'s seminal work on responsibility-driven design. The last entry, by Soukup, is fairly technical but is one of the few books to wrestle with the problem of developing large-scale systems with object technology.

David A. Taylor, *Object-Oriented Technology: A Manager's Guide,* Reading, MA: Addison-Wesley, 1990.

David A. Taylor, *Object-Oriented Information Systems: Planning and Implementation,* New York: John Wiley & Sons, Inc., 1992.

Setrag Khoshafian, A. Brad Baker, Razmik Abnous, and Kevin Shepherd, *Intelligent Offices: Object-Oriented Multi-Media Information Management in Client/Server Architectures,* New York: John Wiley & Sons, Inc., 1992.

Paul Harmon and David A. Taylor, *Objects in Action,* Reading, MA: Addison-Wesley, 1993.

Rebecca Wirfs-Brock, Brian Wilkerson, and Laura Weiner, *Designing Object-Oriented Software,* Englewood Cliffs, NJ: Prentice Hall, 1990.

Brad J. Cox, *Object Oriented Programming: An Evolutionary Approach,* Reading, MA: Addison-Wesley, 1986.

Ivar Jacobson, Magnus Christerson, Patrik Jonsson, and Gunnar Overgaard, *Object-Oriented Software Engineering: A Use Case Driven Approach,* Reading, MA: Addison-Wesley, 1992.

James Rumbaugh, Michael Blaha, William Premerlani, Frederick Eddy, and William Lorensen, *Object-Oriented Modeling and Design,* Englewood Cliffs, NJ: Prentice Hall, 1991.

Grady Booch, *Object-Oriented Design with Applications,* Redwood City, CA: Benjamin/Cummings Publishing Company, Inc., 1991.

James Martin and James J. Odell, *Object-Oriented Analysis and Design,* Englewood Cliffs, NJ: Prentice Hall, 1992.

Jiri Soukup, *Taming C++: Pattern Classes and Persistence for Large Projects,* Reading, MA: Addison-Wesley, 1994.

The Human Element

These last four suggested readings offer insights into human nature and how we can use technology to extend our human capabilities rather than curtail them. The first book presents some insights into the workings of the mind, including the cognitive limitations discussed in Chapter 3. Zuboff's book is a seminal contribution to the understanding of how technology can help people work together more effectively, while Garson's essay demonstrates the harsh contrast between the promise and the reality of computer-supported work. Finally, Schrage's book introduces the powerful idea of linking minds electronically to create a more intelligent organization.

David A. Taylor, *Mind: The Human Difference,* New York: Simon & Schuster, 1982.

Shoshana Zuboff, *In the Age of the Smart Machine: The Future of Work and Power,* New York: Basic Books, 1988.

Barbara Garson, *The Electronic Sweatshop: How Computers Are Transforming the Office of the Future into the Factory of the Past,* New York: Penguin Books, 1988.

Michael Schrage, *Shared Minds: New Technologies of Collaboration,* New York: Random House, 1990.